RACHEL & LEAH

NICKI KOZIARZ

LifeWay Press©
Nashville, Tennessee

EDITORIAL TEAM
ADULT MINISTRY PUBLISHING

Faith Whatley
Director, Adult Ministry

Michelle Hicks
Manager, Adult Ministry
Short Term Bible Studies

Mike Wakefield
Content Editor

Sarah Doss
Production Editor

Heather Wetherington
Art Director

Alexis Ward
Cover Design

STUDENT MINISTRY PUBLISHING

Ben Trueblood
Director, Student Ministry

John Paul Basham
Manager, Student
Ministry Publishing

Karen Daniel
Editorial Team Leader

Drew Dixon
Content Editor

Morgan Hawk
Production Editor

Sarah Nikolai
Graphic Designer

Special thanks to
David Abernathy
Research Assistant

ISBN 978-1-4627-7762-4
Item 005799072
Dewey decimal classification: 248.83
Subject heading: RELIGION/
CHRISTIAN MINISTRY/YOUTH

Unless otherwise noted, all Scripture quotations are taken from the Christian Standard Bible®, Copyright © 2017 by Holman Bible Publishers®. Used by permission. Christian Standard Bible® and CSB® are federally registered trademarks of Holman Bible Publishers. Scripture quotations marked NIV are from THE HOLY BIBLE, NEW INTERNATIONAL VERSION®, NIV® Copyright © 1973, 1978, 1984, 2011 by Biblica, Inc.® Used by permission. All rights reserved worldwide. Scripture quotations marked ESV are from The Holy Bible, English Standard Version® (ESV®), copyright © 2001 by Crossway, a publishing ministry of Good News Publishers. Scripture quotations marked NASB taken from the New American Standard Bible®, Copyright © 1960, 1962, 1963, 1968, 1971, 1972, 1973, 1975, 1977, 1995 by The Lockman Foundation. Used by permission. www.lockman.org.

To order additional copies of this resource, write LifeWay Church Resources Customer Service; One LifeWay Plaza, Nashville, TN 37234; FAX order to 615.251.5933; call toll-free 800.458.2772; email orderentry@lifeway.com; order online at www.lifeway.com; or visit the LifeWay Christian Store serving you.

Printed in the United States of America

Student Ministry Publishing, LifeWay Church Resources
One LifeWay Plaza, Nashville, TN 37234

Contents

About the Author

NICKI KOZIARZ is a wife, mom, author, and speaker with Proverbs 31 Ministries. She and her husband own a fixer-upper farm just outside of Charlotte, NC, where they are raising their girls and barnyard of misfit animals. Nicki speaks nationally at conferences and retreats and is part of the First 5 writer team at Proverbs 31. Visit her website: nickikoziarz.com to connect!

Intro

What will it take for you to say at the end of your life, "It is well with my soul"?[1]

This question began this journey for me. Because things were not well. I was letting something consume my life. It greeted me every morning. And teased me at night. It was there in the mirror. It was there on the scale. It was in the work meeting. It was everywhere.

Comparison.

Feeling less than. Never quite measuring up. Always seeming to be a step behind. And who was I chasing? *Her.*

There is so much to be said about opening the Bible and reading it just as it is. But I've found that when I take my struggles through the Scriptures I uncover a way to become someone I could never be on my own. There is power, authority, and wisdom tucked into the pages of this ancient book we hold in our hands.

Studying the Bible should be an incredible journey that anyone can jump in on. It is a journey filled with answers to questions, some we couldn't even think to ask.

And maybe as we look at this comparison struggle, there's a question you're not sure you've ever really been honest enough to ask. It's this quiet question tucked away in the soul of every girl as she sees beauty, looks at success, and wonders where her happily ever after is.

> This question—Why her?
>
> Why not me?
>
> What's wrong with me?
>
> Who even am I?

As we take a close look at the lives of two women who I consider the two most famous sisters in the Bible, we'll see how all their obsessing over these questions only led to more struggles. We'll note how much each sister lost herself trying to be someone she wasn't. And we'll see what can happen to a woman when she decides to combat comparison God's way.

Each week you'll do five days of personal Bible study. You'll read passages, answer questions, and learn to stop playing the comparison game. Day five will be light and fun as you do some personal insight. All of this will put you on the hunt for who God says you are and who you're going to become with His help.

Each week, you'll study a part of Rachel and Leah's story in a fresh and powerful way and focus on a verse to help you combat comparison. You'll also learn a truth, grounded in the Word of God, that will help you keep comparison from compromising who God created you to be.

Because truth, like always, will set us free. And free girls don't have to measure up to anyone. Not even *her*.

> On a scale of 1-10, (with 1 being unfamiliar and 10 being very knowledgeable), how would you rate your understanding of the story of Rachel and Leah?
>
> 1   2   3   4   5   6   7   8   9   10
>
> What facts do you know about this story? List them below, even if it's just the names of people in the story.

The majority of our study of Rachel and Leah will take place in Genesis 29–31. You're going to be blown away by how much just these three chapters will teach us. Each day you'll begin the study with prayer. I know a lot of times we end our studies in prayer, and we'll do that a few times throughout this journey, but there is something powerful about beginning with prayer. It's that moment when we clear our minds and ask God to step in and teach us only the things He can teach us.

OK, let's go discover how to combat comparison!

Week
One

TRUTH ONE:

You need to be honest.

COMBATING COMPARISON VERSE ONE:
Lord, you have searched me and known me.
PSALM 139:1

Warm Things Up

Ask your group to answer the following questions. This will help you begin to build much needed community for this study!

What made you decide to be a part of this study?

What are some hopes/expectations you have for this study?

Where do you like to do your Bible study?

What tends to distract and detour you away from doing Bible study?

Watch

To hear more from Nicki, download the optional video bundle to view the Week One teaching at www.lifeway.com/RachelandLeah.

Create Conversation

If there is one thing you could change about yourself, what would it be? Does this desired change come from healthy motivation or is it driven by comparison? Explain.

What is the quiet question we ask when we compare ourselves to others? Share about a time you've found yourself asking this.

How have you personally experienced the negative consequences of comparison? In what areas of your life are you prone to compare?

What three things did Nicki challenge you to do this week? Which of these three will be most difficult for you? Explain.

How will you combat comparison with the truth of Psalm 139:1 this week?

End your time together by praying for the girls in your group to have the freedom and trust to be honest before the Lord, with themselves, and with the group.

Video sessions available for purchase at www.lifeway.com/RachelandLeah

And So It Begins

Jacob resumed his journey and went to the eastern country.
He looked and saw a well in a field.
GENESIS 29:1-2a

Beginning Prayer:
Before you begin each study,
jot down a personal prayer here.

_____

_____

_____

Every journey begins with the first step. And today, we take
our first step into an ancient text to begin discovering one of
the most fascinating stories in the Bible. This story is filled with
drama, mouth-dropping statements, and details that will literally
make your eyes bulge. But it's also a love story, a redemption
story, and ultimately a God-story.

GRAB YOUR BIBLE AND READ GENESIS 29:1-3.

One of the best things we can do after reading a verse or verses is to start asking questions.

What questions can you think of to ask about these three verses?

Here are few questions I'm asking:

Who is Jacob?

What is this journey he's on?

Where is this well in a field?

We may or may not be able to answer all our questions throughout this journey. There are some questions the Bible just flat out leaves mysterious. Questions that leave us with more questions. And answers that don't seem to really answer. But for today, let's start with what I think is the most important question from these three verses:

Who is Jacob?

A few months ago, I was meeting with some new people for an informational meeting at a little coffee shop in my small town. After I got my coffee, I walked over toward two women sitting in the corner and asked if they were there for the same meeting. They replied with a quick *yes,* but continued their conversation completely ignoring me.

Unsure if I was interrupting them, I pulled one of the other chairs at the table away from them and sat down, as if the space made some type of emotional barrier between us. It didn't work, but at least I tried.

Getting more insecure by the moment, I tried to grasp what they were talking about so I could jump into the conversation. They mentioned a name that was familiar to me, so I jumped in, "Oh, I know her!"

They both looked at me with the strangest look, until one of them replied in a rather snobbish tone, "Her, is a him."

Ahem. Blush.

Obviously, I stopped trying to figure out who they were talking about and just sat quietly, feeling like a complete fool.

As awkward as that situation was, I was reminded how important it is to know the context of a situation. We can't always just jump into conversations and know what's going on.

Similarly we shouldn't jump into the middle of a book of the Bible and assume we know what's going on. Taking the time to understand what's happening where we pick up in the story, understanding who is who, and studying a story inside and out is so valuable. If we want to understand what's *really* happening in a passage, we need to examine its context.

God is not concerned with how much we know or don't know. He doesn't care where we jump into the story. But usually we gain a deeper understanding of the story by learning more of the background. God is the best teacher—always welcoming our questions, our curiosity, and even our doubt. There's never a snobby response back from Him if we get something wrong or don't understand things.

What we gain from understanding the whole picture of what we are studying is amazing. When I first read Jacob's name, I thought I knew a lot about him. But what I discovered was fascinating.

> Let's figure out who Jacob was. Turn to Genesis 25:19-28. Read those verses and then answer these questions:
>
> 1. Jacob's mother and father were named _____ and _____.
>
> 2. Circle the correct answer:
>   A. Jacob was three years older than his brother.
>   B. Jacob was five years younger than his brother.
>   C. Esau and Jacob were twins.
>
> 3. How old was Isaac when they were born?
>
> 4. What does it say the boys grew up to do?
>   Esau:
>
>
>   Jacob:

5. According to verse 28, why did Isaac love Esau?

6. Does the text say why Rebekah loved Jacob?

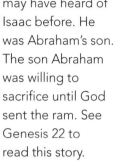

FAST FACT: You may have heard of Isaac before. He was Abraham's son. The son Abraham was willing to sacrifice until God sent the ram. See Genesis 22 to read this story.

7. What are your thoughts about what seems to be a confession of who was who's favorite child?

Comparison is already rearing it's ugly head in this journey. These two boys is where it begins, but it will be a thread throughout the entire process.

Tomorrow we're going to dig into Jacob's journey. But for now, I want to talk about your journey and share a little bit more about mine.

For way too long comparison stole so much from me. It made me miss out on the special, unique, and incredible plans God had for my life. It made me look to the left and to the right, missing what was right in front of me. And I just felt miserable. My license plate could have read, *Unhappiest Woman in America.*

I have a feeling you've had a moment or two like this in your life too. Because no matter how confident you are, you've been compared and you've done the comparing. None of us are exempt from this struggle. But what I've discovered about most girls is that we love to shout our success, but seldom speak of our sorrows.

And battling comparison, unlike wanting to quit, being disorganized, or not having it all together, is something we rarely admit.

Maybe you haven't allowed yourself to admit to the struggle of comparison in your life. Or maybe you're so fed up with this struggle you are ready to suffocate it. But we're here. Together. Ready to do the best we can do to combat this comparison compromise.

Circle all the areas where comparison has tried to take you captive:

School *Activities* *Body Image* *Social Media* *Sports*
Grades *Clothing* *Success* *Friends* *Relationships*

Are there other areas? Let's get honest about them, right here, right now. This is just between you and God. List any other specific areas where you are struggling with comparison:

TURN TO 2 CORINTHIANS 10:12.

What does this verse say happens when we compare ourselves with others?

What are some of the effects comparison has had on you? On your attitude? Your behavior? Your confidence?

As we wrap up this first day of study, I want us to take a minute to process a few things. By the end of this study, I hope you have a deeper understanding of how God thinks of you. When we shift our minds to knowing what God says and thinks about us, we'll shift not only our thinking, but the words we use to describe ourselves.

I want to help you build holy confidence. That's why I'm giving you six truths and six Combating Comparison Verses throughout this study.

Go back to the first page of this week's study.

Write out Truth One:

Write out our Combating Comparison Verse One:

Throughout the week we'll spend some time processing Truth One, but today I want you to process this verse.

1. Read Psalm 139:1-7 to get the full context of this verse.
   *Bonus study, read all of Psalm 139.

2. Do an Internet search to find out who the author of this psalm was. The author was _____.

3. What do you think would have made this verse significant for the author's life?

4. What does it mean to you to know that God knows everything about you?

OK friend, that's a wrap for Day One. See you tomorrow as we learn more about Jacob's role in this tale of two sisters.

He Just Had to Go

Jacob asked the men at the well, "My brothers! Where are you from?"
"We're from Haran," they answered. "Do you know Laban grandson
of Nahor?" Jacob asked them. They answered, "We know him."
GENESIS 29:4-5

Beginning Prayer:

_____

_____

_____

Can you think of the most defining moment of your life so far? A moment
when everything shifted in an instant and nothing was ever the same?

Of course, the moment we invite Jesus into our lives should always be the most defining, but
I'm talking about moments where decisions defined us, maybe in a not-so-great way.

It's these moments where life is never the same again. We've all had them. Some more
dramatic than others, but they are there. I remember one of the most significant defining
moments in my life very clearly.

Nineteen. Alone. Standing in a bathroom holding a pregnancy test that read "positive."
My life shifted instantly. That moment was defining because while I had struggled with
comparison for what seemed like a lifetime, becoming a mom at such a young age wasn't
exactly ideal material for learning to become comfortable in your own skin.

I spent a lot of my early twenties looking at all these women who seemed to have life way
more figured out than I did. Comparison convinces us we're failures. And our failures
leave us in a place of constant comparison. It's this cycle that never seems to go away.

But failure in life is really one of life's greatest teachers. And it's time for you and me to
get honest about our failures. There's so much God wants to teach us about our past. It
contains clues to help us understand what's happening today.

Describe the first time comparison showed up in your life:

How has comparison played a role in a significant failure in your life?

What are some examples of ways students in your school or community engage in comparison?

Yesterday we saw Jacob and Esau's own parents showing favoritism. For sure, a defining moment in both of their journeys. How do the comparisons we face as children affect defining moments in the future?

Yesterday we learned a little bit about Jacob. He's a significant part of this story we're studying, so as we jump back into our story, we need to uncover a few more defining moments for Jacob.

Arriving at the well was a defining moment in his journey. But you might be wondering, *what he's doing at this well anyway?*

Let's do some digging.

READ GENESIS 25:27-34.

What does Esau call the meal Jacob was making?

What did Jacob ask Esau to sell him (v. 31)?

> **FAST FACT**
> **BIRTHRIGHT:**
> The firstborn son was given special privileges and duties in the family. He also received a double portion of the inheritance.[1] For Esau to sell his birthright for a pot of beans would have been equivalent to selling your grandmother's two-carat diamond ring for a bowl of Cheerios. Not worth it.

> **FAST FACT:** Isaac went on to live over forty years after this incident.[4]

What role would comparison have played during this defining moment for Jacob and Esau?

This was a big defining moment for both Jacob and Esau. Nothing would ever be the same between them again. But this intense struggle to be the best didn't end there. In fact, we'll see it get worse a few verses later. It's a constant theme throughout their story.

Isaac became old and unable to see well (Gen. 27:1). He became weak and sick and thought his days might be up very soon. So he asked Esau to go out and catch something yummy to eat. Isaac wanted this to be a special moment between him and Esau in which he could give Esau his blessing (Gen. 27:2-4).

The blessing was different than the birthright. The birthright was what they were required to get by law, such as the double portion of the inheritance.[2] The blessing is what the father decided to give, such as who would become head of the extended family after the father's death.[3] So what Jacob did next was extra shady. He went to Isaac and pretended to be Esau, and Isaac fell for it (Gen. 27:27-29).

And whoa, did this stir up some anger in Esau. Once Isaac and Rebecca saw how in danger both of their lives were, they made a drastic decision.

READ GENESIS 27:41–28:2.

Where did Rebecca tell Jacob to go?

What did Isaac tell Jacob to do there?

Circle the reason why Rebecca and Isaac told Jacob to do this:

    A. To calm down

    B. To find a wife

    C. To hide from Esau

    D. All of the above

Turn to Genesis 28:10. On the map below, draw an arrow from Jacob's starting point to his ending point.

Does Genesis 29:1-4 tell us how long it took Jacob to arrive at the well? Yes or No

That's about like walking from Charlotte, NC, to Orlando, FL, or from San Diego to San Francisco.

As we wrap up today's study, I want us to think about our starting point and where we want to end up. Bible studies are great, but just knowing a lot about the Bible isn't going to change our lives. It's when we apply God's Word to our attitude and actions that we see the most impact.

For many of us, comparison has a hold on our lives in a way that has caused us to pause. We've become numb to believing God has special, unique things just for us.

In Romans 12:4-8, we see the genius of God's design in putting all of us together in the church, each with a part to play and a gift to contribute, but none able to go it alone. He could have appointed just a few superwomen and supermen to do it all, but He didn't. If we are willing to just do our part and not compare how our part measures up to someone else's, we just might find the thrill of being a functioning part of a something much larger than ourselves. Plus, we'll likely come away with some great relationships added in for good measure.

Tomorrow, we'll discover a key turning point in Jacob's story. But today, I believe is a turning point for you and me. The more unsettled we allow ourselves to become with this comparison struggle, the more likely we are to overcome it. And the more honest we get about where we are, the more we'll see where we need to go. It's the struggles we hide or simply deny that never see the light of victory.

I want you to fill in this timeline of your comparison struggles. The starting point is where this whole issue first popped up in your life. But where will it end?

Jacob knew his destination was Haran. He didn't know what was in store for him there, but it was better than where he was.

And where God wants you and me to end up is much better than where we are now. He wants your destination to be freedom.

Take a few minutes to plot out your comparison journey. Here are some questions you might want to consider:

- What is your first memory of comparison?
- What were some of your "defining moments"?
- Who has been your biggest internal rival?
- What are the lessons you've learned along the way?
- What has God revealed to you about this struggle?

Your Comparison Journey

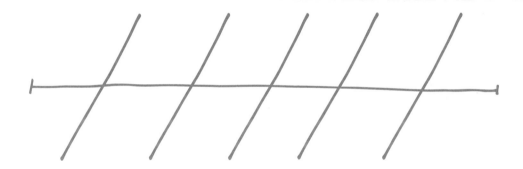

As you think about the end: What do you want your life free of comparison to look like? How will your life be different?

What are some practical steps you can take to move closer to freedom? I've filled in a few for you. Add in some specific steps of your own to your journey below:

- Daily time with God
- Surrounding yourself with Christian friends who will help you grow
- Replacing my comparison thoughts with a Combating Comparison Verse
- Staying focused on where I want to end up in life, not where others are headed
- Learning to express gratitude for what I have
-
-
-
-
-
-
-

I'm proud of you for taking the time to really work through this! I'll see you tomorrow as we continue our journey.

MID-WEEK TRUTH CHECK-IN

TRUTH ONE:
You need to be honest.

Each week I'm giving you a truth your soul needs to hear to help combat comparison. These truths, lined up with God's Word, will give us the strength to fight this internal enemy a little more each day.

Our first truth: **You need to be honest.**

I know this sounds incredibly basic, and maybe you're rolling your eyes at this not-so-profound truth. It's simple. Yes. But until we are honest with ourselves and others about our struggle with comparison, we'll continue to live in denial. Knowing truth and living truth are two different things.

It's time to dismiss denial and dishonesty and invite honesty to transform us.

Today, we're going to start applying Scripture to this week's Truth.

Fill in the blanks for our verse this week:
Lord, _____ have _____ me and _____ me.
(Psalm 139:1).

Read and write down Psalm 139:23 as a prayer for this time of reflection.

If we have thoughts and emotions that we know are not pleasing to God, the best way to get rid of them is to ask Him to search us. We can't hide from God, but this is a good thing. The kindness of His presence often brings us to a place of repentance.

When you think about the idea of God searching your heart right now, what is something you might be fearful of Him seeing in you when it comes to this struggle of comparison?

What are the good things God would see in your heart?

What are the longings or desires God sees in your heart?

There She Comes

"Do you know Laban grandson of Nahor?" Jacob asked them.
They answered, "We know him." "Is he well?" Jacob asked.
"Yes," they said, "and here is his daughter Rachel,
coming with his sheep."
GENESIS 29:5-6

Beginning Prayer:

_____

_____

_____

If there was a playlist for this study, I'd have you start the lesson by listening to Manfred Mann's "Doo Wha Diddy Diddy."[6] I know it's an old song, but it's really fun. I totally give you permission to pause today's study and have a little dance party. It was the first song that popped in my head when I read the verses we are going to be unpacking today.

If Jacob had known that song, I bet it would have popped into his head on this hot day at a well in Haran.

I once read that people make their judgments of you within seven seconds of meeting you.[7] That's not a lot of time! Maybe that's why people spend so much time on their clothes, makeup, hair, and such. Or maybe it's because we want to come off a little more impressive than we really are.

We're about to meet someone named Rachel, the daughter of a man named, Laban. As she got up that morning, brushed her hair, and picked out her clothes, she had no idea what was coming. If she had known, she might have spent a few extra moments getting ready. This day was going to be a defining moment for her.

> **LABAN FAST FACTS:**
> Brother to Jacob's mom, Rebekah.
> First mentioned in Genesis 24:29-60. His occupation: Farmer.

READ GENESIS 29:5-9.

Have you ever heard of Laban before? Yes or No

Who does verse 5 say Laban's grandfather was?

TURN TO GENESIS 11:26.

Who was one of the grandfather's brothers? Circle the right answer.
A. Isaac
B. Joseph
C. Abram

In verse 7, why was Jacob so surprised Rachel was bringing her sheep to the well?

> **FUN FACT:**
> Rachel is the first shepherdess mentioned in the Bible.[9]

I'm not sure we can make much of a point about the time of day they were coming to the well. They might have done things a lot differently 500 miles away where Jacob was from. One commentary suggests that perhaps Jacob was trying to get the herdsmen to go away so he could talk with Rachel.[8]

What was Rachel's job?

I love this moment when Rachel walked up to the well. It's a beautiful, sovereign moment. It reminds us that life is full of unexpected moments. Normally we think of these unexpected things in a bad way—spilling food on your shirt during lunch, being tardy for first period, or running laps at practice.

God has the best surprises in life for us. But comparison keeps our eyes on ourselves and causes us to miss what's happening right in front of us. The more honest we become, the better we'll get to a place where we reject comparison and receive confidence.

Jacob also needed to get honest with himself and with God. We have seen a few of his dishonest struggles unfold. But Jacob had a big defining moment before he arrived at this well—an encounter with God.

Sometimes encounters with God leave us warm and fuzzy, and sometimes they leave us with a desire to do some deep soul-searching.

While Jacob was traveling from Beer-sheba to Haran, he had to take a break to sleep. Something incredible happened while he was asleep.

READ GENESIS 28:10-22.

What did Jacob use to lay his head on?

FAST FACT:
There are twenty-one dreams recorded in the Bible.[10]

Describe his dream:

What did Jacob name this place?

What vow did Jacob make?
    A. That he would apologize to Esau
    B. That he would give God a tenth of everything
    C. That he would find a wife
    D. That he would never lie again

In this fast-paced world, we find ourselves running through each day. It's hard to create space for encounters with God. There's so much information buzzing in our brains all day.

Sometimes God gifts us with the grace of honesty by being in His presence. We are able to see ourselves in the light of truth. This honest assessment helps keep our mistakes from turning into a failure-filled future.

Describe a time you had an undeniable encounter with God:

Turn to John 10:14 and fill in the blanks:
"I am the _____ _____ ."

Wait. Are you seeing what I'm seeing? Jacob had this undeniable encounter with God which led to this amazing providential moment at the well—where there are literally sheep showing up! God, the Good Shepherd, has guided Jacob to this exact moment.

But it only came after one of the most gut-level honest moments Jacob had with God. There were things God needed to show Jacob that were keeping him from experiencing all that He had for him.

And I'm so sorry to tell you this, but until the day we arrive in heaven, we are also in this process where God needs to reveal the sin in our hearts. Comparison has compromised a lot of things in our lives. It may not be our only struggle, but it's the root of a lot of them.

Yesterday I wanted you to get a taste of what it would be like to be a little more free from this comparison struggle. Today, as we wrap up this idea of being honest with yourself and with God, take time to realize where you are in the process. Remember how Jacob's defining moment led to the next step in his journey.

Here's a prayer I'm praying for both of us:

Father, as we lean into this story of Jacob's redefining moment, we know that you have redefining moments for each of us. We ask you to show us our Bethel, the place where we have an undeniable encounter with You, which leads to the beginning of our struggles ending. Holy Spirit, reveal what needs to be revealed and give us the gift of grace wrapped in honesty.

Awkward Entries

Then Jacob kissed Rachel and wept loudly.
GENESIS 29:11

Beginning Prayer:

_____

_____

_____

I seem to be the queen of awkward entries. I've had a slew of them in my lifetime. But the worst example was probably the time I walked into a room full of people and fell flat on my face.

That morning, I was running late for an event where I was teaching and grabbed the first pair of shoes I could find, white sandals. It had rained that morning and the parking lot was full of puddles. Rushing into the building, my feet splashed in puddle after puddle. When I came dashing into the room, my wet shoes met with the recently waxed floors. My first introduction was my face to the floor. No one in the room knew what to do, and it became one of the most awkward moments of my entire life.

I'm sure you've had a moment or two like this. Please, tell me you have?

As we pick back up with our story, Jacob is about to have his own little awkward entry.

READ GENESIS 29:9-11.

According to verse 10, what does Jacob do as soon as he sees Rachel?

I smile when I picture this moment. Because men will always be men. Maybe Jacob was being a perfect gentlemen, or maybe he was being a little bit of a show-off. As you can see from the picture, removing this stone wasn't like popping the lid off a spaghetti sauce jar. It took a lot of strength.

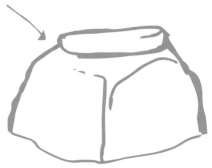

LARGE STONE LID

Most of the commentaries I studied said there were probably several reasons why the well was covered up in the first place. It could have been because they didn't want any sheep falling in.[11] Or it might have been designed to protect the well,[12] to keep it from drying up or becoming contaminated.[13]

Whatever the reason, the stone was heavy. It would take a strong man to move it. Perhaps Jacob was ready to show Rachel that he had the strength to move it.

> Go back and read Genesis 29:2. How many flocks of sheep does it say were already at the well?
>
> A. 5
> B. 10
> C. 3
>
> Why do you think the other shepherds hadn't already moved the stone to water their sheep? Circle the best answer:
>
> A. They were being lazy.
> B. The stone was too heavy.
> C. It was too hot.
> D. They were waiting for all the flocks to arrive so the water wouldn't get contaminated.

Honestly, it could have been a number of reasons. We don't know one hundred percent. But what we do know is Jacob took the initiative and moved the stone.

A little showing off isn't too out of character for a man, even in today's society. But what happens next puzzles me a bit.

READ GENESIS 29:11.

Write what it says Jacob did:

This is one of the places in Scripture we need to look a little closer to really understand what's happening. Yes, Jacob just straight-up kissed Rachel. But this wasn't a big, romantic, smoochy-type kiss. It was a common way to greet someone in Jacob's culture.

When I first met my husband's family, I felt really uncomfortable. Every time we would say goodbye to them, they would kiss me on the cheek. And I was like, "Um, ya, I don't even know you, this is weird." I'm not a real touchy person. I like my personal space, and it just felt really awkward to say goodbye to someone like this … for *years*.

But my husband's family is made up of people who transplanted to the South. They are originally from New York. And this is a very common thing for people to do up there. But for us Southerners, it feels strange. We're huggers, mostly side huggers. But after understanding their background and their upbringing, it made me feel less uncomfortable. What is called "kissing" in much of the world does not involve a lot of physical contact. It's the "air kiss" just to the side of the face. In some places (like Ethiopia) there are three kisses—one on one side, one on the other side, and then another kiss back on the first side.

What are some other cultural differences you can think of across the United States or the world?

So maybe we can wrap our minds around the kissing, but Jacob's crying?

Why do you think Jacob wept when he saw Rachel?

I'm guessing it was a combination of things. "Jacob was a quiet man, dwelling in tents" (Gen 25:27, ESV). He stayed at home, so he probably was not a traveler. So after he had just completed a 500 mile journey, he would have been exhausted and lonely. He was probably also wondering if he would find his mother's family so far away from home, and if there would be anyone there he could marry. So perhaps the combination of fatigue, loneliness, and anxiety made him especially emotional. Then when he saw a relative, his mother's niece, he was overjoyed.

READ GENESIS 29:12.

What was Rachel's response?

Something made her eager to get home quickly to her father. I don't know, maybe this was an answer to Rachel's hopes and dreams. Maybe she was in shock. Whatever it was, nothing would ever be the same for Rachel and her family from this moment on. Another defining moment on the story radar.

We've built the foundation for our story this week. And today is where we end our study of Rachel and Leah for the week. Tomorrow, we begin our study of *you*. That's right, friend. I'm so excited to help you uncover all the unique and incredible things about who God has created you to be.

As we wrap up this week's study of Rachel and Leah, I want you to remember the key points.

List all the characters we were introduced to this week. (Hint, there are five people and one group of people):

List at least three defining moments we've uncovered in this story:

1.

2.

3.

How did our Combating Comparison Verse of the week (Psalm 139:1) help you uncover your comparison battle?

OK! High-fives. You did it. One week of study complete.

You Be You

What kind of Bible study girl are you?

1. Your favorite type of Bible studies are:
    A. Verse-by-verse studies through a book of the Bible
    B. Studies on faith, courage, and victory
    C. Anything in the Psalms
    D. Anything in Proverbs

2. You participate in class by:
    A. Listening carefully
    B. Offering new ideas or new perspectives
    C. Affirming/agreeing with others in their responses
    D. Having an answer prepared in case you're called on

3. You'll do your homework:
    A. Carefully, slowly, and thoughtfully
    B. While also checking in with the other girls in class
    C. At the same time each day
    D. Honestly, you might not, but if you do, it'll be deep

4. When you look at your Bible study book or page:
    A. It contains others' prayer requests that you jotted down
    B. You've got action steps or things you want to do
    C. It's neat and tidy
    D. You have other verses on the same subject in the sidebar

5. If you have a question during the week, you will:
    A. Text a friend from class
    B. Dig into the Greek or Hebrew definitions
    C. Creatively come up with a few different answers
    D. Look it up on the Internet

RESULTS:

Question 1	Question 2	Question 3	Question 4	Question 5
A) 1	A) 4	A) 4	A) 3	A) 3
B) 2	B) 2	B) 3	B) 2	B) 4
C) 3	C) 3	C) 1	C) 1	C) 2
D) 4	D) 1	D) 2	D) 4	D) 1

Mostly 1s

You are the Delightfully Devoted Bible Study Girl!

On time and ready to go, you are consistent. You find joy in having every page complete and every blank filled in. Other girls can count on you.

Mostly 2s

You are the True Trailblazer Bible Study Girl!

You've got ideas! You've got guts! You are ready to inspire! It's hard to hold you back during Bible Study. Your input and enthusiasm are epic!

Mostly 3s

You are the Cheerful Encourager Bible Study Girl!

You want to be positive and build others up. You enjoy fellowship, hugs, and conversation. You will be the first to pass the tissues if someone starts crying.

Mostly 4s

You are the Wise Observer Bible Study Girl!

You are a serious scholar and deep thinker. You like to mull things over and hear other people's responses before chiming in. You keep the group anchored.

Week
Two

TRUTH TWO:

See it like it really is.

COMBATING COMPARISON VERSE TWO:
*Charm is deceptive and beauty is fleeting,
but a woman who fears the L*ORD *will be praised.*
PROVERBS 31:30

Warm Things Up

Here are a few questions to get your group talking.

What are some things you learned from this week's personal study?

How did comparison show up in your life this week?

What did you learn from plotting out your comparison journey?

Share a personal defining moment and how it shaped your life.

How have you applied the Combating Comparison Verse this week?

Watch

To hear more from Nicki, download the optional video bundle to view the Week Two teaching at www.LifeWay.com/RachelandLeah.

Create Conversation

Truth Two: _____ it like it _____ is.

Sometimes we don't _____ things for what they really _____.

Do you ever have trouble seeing things like they really are? Explain.

How do God's Word and prayer help you see things as they really are?

When you hear the phrase "fear of the Lord," what comes to mind? What would it look like practically to walk in the fear of the Lord?

What are some ways Nicki suggests that you can cultivate "fear of the Lord" in your heart?

Close by praying that the girls in your group would have the desire and ability to see God for who He is and to see things as they really are.

Oh, Sister

Now Laban had two daughters: the older was named Leah,
and the younger was named Rachel. Leah had tender eyes,
but Rachel was shapely and beautiful.

GENESIS 29:16-17

Beginning Prayer:
Before you begin each study,
jot down a personal prayer here.

If you could have seen me last night, you probably would have laughed.

I pretty much looked like an infomercial going to bed. On my nightstand was a pink rock, with promises of clearing the air. My feet were cradled in soft, fuzzy socks with promises of making my feet baby soft. I dabbed some essential oils behind my ears, with promises of giving me the deepest sleep possible. In my hair were soft-fabric rollers that came with the assurance of never having to blow dry my hair again. And on my face was a cream that promised to make all my wrinkles and sunspots disappear overnight.

Oh yes, I've bought into all the beauty promises, my friends. Because who doesn't want to believe that there's something we can do to make ourselves look and feel better?

Advertisers are onto us, girls. It's estimated that a woman will spend $15,000 on beauty products in her lifetime.[1] And still, every time we see a girl more beautiful than us there's something inside of us that whispers, *"Why don't I look like that?"*

But it's not just us whispering these things. There's an entire world telling us what we are and what we aren't. And yes, we could just say, *don't listen to them.* But the truth is that we live in a world that is constantly encouraging us to compare ourselves to others.

Today we'll see something in the Bible that I don't love. That's right. I said I don't love something about the Bible. Well, really something Moses, the author of Genesis, wrote.

Because you guys, we're going to read the words he wrote about this woman, and while they aren't rude, they definitely are not kind.

READ GENESIS 29:13-17.

How does verse 17 describe Rachel? _____

And Leah? _____

OK, so it's not like Moses is chanting the old cheer, that unfortunately, you're probably familiar with:

"U-G-L-Y! You ain't got no alibi, you ugly, hey, hey … you ugly."[2]

But he's being very generous in the way Rachel is described. And not so much with Leah. There are a dozen opinions on what exactly the text means by "tender eyes." Some scholars say it means her eyes were weak,[3] crossed,[4] or dull.[5]

Whatever it means, we know this: Rachel is described as shapely and beautiful, Leah is not.

Here's another little not-so-amazing thing about these sisters. Rachel's name means *ewe*,[6] which is another word for a sheep. Leah's name? Well, it means *cow*.[7] But before we get all upset with their parents, there's more to this story.

Most parents spend a lot of time considering the name of their child. They want it to be something meaningful and important to them. Laban, the girl's father, was a farmer, so animals were important to him. He was surrounded by them. They were part of his daily vocabulary.

But, still. A name that means *cow*? Mmm. I don't know how Leah felt about *that*. Especially all those years she spent in her beautiful sister's shadow.

If I were making a list of all the things that women compare themselves over, I can assure you, looks would be at the top of that list. This is the first form of comparison we see in this story. And of all the places, *in the Bible*.

Why do you think girls are compared by their appearances so much?

List of as many ways you can think of that girls compare appearances with each other (ex: hairstyles, makeup, etc.):

What do you think makes someone beautiful?

Beauty is in the eyes of the beholder. So the question is, who are you letting behold your beauty? The world? Others? Or yourself?

Fill in the blanks for this week's Combating Comparison Verse:
Charm is _____ and _____ is fleeting, but a _____ who _____ the LORD will be _____ .
Proverbs 31:30

This verse is a gift to those of us struggling with feeling like we'll never measure up with our looks. Because the reality is, someone will always be more beautiful than us. But God reveals to us something that lasts longer than a perfect face or body.

READ PSALM 34:11,13-14; 111:10; AND PROVERBS 1:7.

What does it mean to "fear the Lord"?

Why did I look like an infomercial last night? Because yes, I compare my looks too. I see women who are thinner, their skin is flawless, and they always look so put together. I want that too. And I often believe the lie that if I could just have this one "magical" product, with all of its promises, it would make me better. Then I wouldn't compare anymore.

But most of the time those promise-filled products just leave me feeling like an item on the clearance rack—*picked over.*

I'm wondering what Rachel and Leah's childhood was like. Was Rachel always described as the pretty one? Did Leah always feel less than her sister?

This passage isn't giving us a lot of background information, but I found something interesting while studying. During this time period, mirrors were not a thing. The only reflection they were able to see was in water or some type of glass.[8]

They weren't waking up each morning with an instant unwanted greeting from the mirror telling them how unlovely they looked. They weren't spending hours and hours in front of the mirror each morning perfecting that YouTube makeup how-to tutorial, blow-drying, straightening and curling hair, or plucking eyebrows.

I imagine their getting ready process was very short and simple.

Wake up.

Go to the bathroom. (Because some struggles are timeless.)

Put on clothes and sandals.

Splash some water on the face.

Tuck hair into shawl.

And go.

Can you imagine what they would think of our morning routines in this 21st century world we live in? Good grief.

While they weren't going through the daily mirror comparison, obviously they still struggled with comparison and had to endure being compared by others.

READ GENESIS 29:18-19.

Fill in the blanks:

Jacob _____ Rachel.

He promised to work _____ years for her hand in marriage.

How did Laban respond?

Cousin-marriage was indeed somewhat common during this time. In fact, it was encouraged because the population was small, and there weren't many choices. Even today cousin-marriage is a preferred arrangement in many traditional societies, especially among Muslims (who draw heavily from middle-eastern cultural patterns, partly because of the Arabic cultural background of Islam).[11]

In Pakistan, 70 percent of all marriages are cousin-marriages.[12] They are also fairly common in much of the rest of the Muslim world.[13] It keeps families together because there are already bonds of loyalty and relationship. It also keeps family wealth, more or less, in the family.[14]

Why did Jacob have to do anything besides propose to be able to marry Rachel?

While today, it is courteous of a man to ask the father of the woman he loves for her hand in marriage, it's definitely not required (*except in my house—take note future sons-in-law*). But during this time-period, it was not only required to ask the father for permission, but the man had to be prepared with something called a Bride Price. This isn't to be confused with "purchasing a wife." It was a different custom.

Bible scholar John Walton describes it like this:

> *The agreement reached between Laban and Jacob is intended to provide for the bride price that was an essential part of marriage contracts. This was a payment made from the groom or his family to the family of the bride. Its function was to serve as a trust fund of sorts to provide for the support of the wife should the husband divorce her or die.[15]*

What does Genesis 29:18 say Jacob wanted?

How many years was he willing to work?

A. 10

B. 15

C. 7

D. 1

Jacob's offer of seven years of work for Laban was very generous.[16] Maybe even a little over the top. In fact, Laban struck a gold mine in Jacob's offer. Someone else might have offered half that much.[17]

Why do you think Jacob made such a generous offer for Rachel?

How do you think it made Leah feel to hear of Jacob's offer for Rachel? Describe any "behind-the-scenes" conversations that might have taken place.

We'll see later on some of Rachel's and Leah's character traits which reveal the unhealthy tension between these sisters. One that must have started long before Jacob came walking into town.

Think through what a sister-sister relationship is really like. What could have been some ways comparison showed up between Rachel and Leah before this point?

That's one of the tricky things about comparison. It can start sowing its seeds in a season we don't think really matters. But then it grows and grows, one day turning into a huge mess. For us. For someone else. And ultimately for our assignment from God.

We're in for a big plot twist in this story tomorrow. Stay tuned.

Plot Twist

When morning came, there was Leah!
GENESIS 29:25a

Beginning Prayer:

_____

_____

_____

What are some of the ingredients that would make for a perfect wedding day? The right venue? Food? Weather?

A few weeks ago, our fixer-upper farm hosted its first wedding. It's always been a dream of mine to host weddings, but it's a pretty complicated and expensive process to become a wedding venue. So we never really pursued it.

But when my friend mentioned her sister was planning a very small, simple wedding but was having a hard time finding an outdoor venue, I offered up our farm. It seemed like a perfect fit to try out this process.

I think I was more excited about the wedding than anyone. We spent hours and hours cutting the grass just right, cleaning up bushes, making the front porch lovely. And the bride had the most beautiful wooden arch to display in the yard.

I even got to play wedding coordinator, telling everyone when to head down the aisle and making sure someone pressed play for the music. Except for a few fire ants, it really was a perfect day.

I know not everyone's wedding day is as flawless as that one was. There have been so many viral videos showing brides' dresses catching on fire, grooms passing out, and ministers making mistakes during the vows. But I'm not sure much could compare to this wedding mishap we're about to discover.

READ GENESIS 29:21-23.

What was Jacob's request of Laban in verse 21?

Commentaries say that the wording of Jacob's statement to Laban was kind of pushy and demanding. I guess maybe he felt he had paid his dues and had the right to demand to have Rachel.[18]

How did Laban respond?

Who did Laban invite to the feast?
   A. The town elders
   B. Everyone who wanted to come
   C. The men
   D. Only his family

What time of day was it?

READ GENESIS 29:23-25.

I know. You're thinking the same thing I am. How on earth does someone not recognize the person they are marrying!?

Well, chances are there had been quite a bit of alcohol involved before, during, and after the ceremony, as would have been custom.[19] And it was evening, so it was dark. But also, Leah had to have a veil over her face.[20]

But where was Rachel when all of this was happening? The text doesn't tell us anything about whether or not she was there or what she was feeling in this moment. But can you imagine how awful this must have been for her? To be in love. To plan a wedding. To be tricked by her own dad and sister!

And then there's Leah. The primary deception was Laban's, but Leah has some responsibility as well. What would her motivation have been? Part of it may simply have been complying with her father's will, but I suspect that she may have begun to feel that she was not going to be spoken for—at least not with Laban at the controls, manipulating everything to his own advantage. She could have been thinking, *This is probably the only chance I will ever have, so I'll go along with it, even though I know it isn't exactly right. The important thing is that I get a man out of it.*

Regardless, I don't think being in this situation brought her one ounce of joy.

If I were in a situation like Leah's, I'm not sure I would have been able to sleep a wink that night. I would be dreading the next morning so much. My thoughts would have been running faster than a freight train the entire night: *What will Jacob say? Will he change his mind about how he feels about Rachel? Will he think I'm suitable for him?*

What other thoughts might Leah have wrestled with that night?

But eventually the sun rose. Light poured in through the cracks in the tent, and the truth was revealed. Jacob had the surprise of his life. Instead of Rachel, there was Leah.

How does Genesis 29:25 describe Jacob's reaction?

Talk about ironic! Let's look back at another situation of someone pretending to be someone they weren't.

READ GENESIS 27:18-24.

Who did Jacob pretend to be?

Why did Issac question which son was speaking to him?

READ GENESIS 27:41.

How did Esau react? What does this tell you about him?

What parallels do you see in the two deception stories?

"You will reap what you sow," isn't just something we say when someone is paid back for the way they behaved—this phrase is found in Scripture. Our faith is deeply rooted around the golden rule. The Bible constantly reminds us that our actions have consequences (2 Cor. 9:6; Prov. 11:18; Gal. 6:7-8), and we should give careful thought to the impact of our actions.

READ LUKE 6:31 AND FILL IN THE BLANKS:

Just as you _____ others to _____ for you, do the _____ for _____.

What does Galatians 6:7 say God cannot be?

    A. Seen

    B. Mocked

    C. Lied to

How do you sow "good" seed into your life?

What is an example from your life of a "comes around goes around" moment, good or bad?

There is only one thing in your life that never becomes void despite any decision, choice, or action you take. That, my friend, is the love of God. It has and always will be a constant in your life. There is no coming or going around His unconditional love.

Understand that the decisions we are making today are directing the outcome of our tomorrows. The people we are kind to, love well, and the decisions we make, all determine how our lives will be looked back on.

I call this mind-set your "rocking chair" moment.

Let's say you've lived as much life as possible and you're sitting on your front porch in a rocker. Rocking and thinking about all you've done and accomplished. What are those things? But more importantly, who are the people surrounding you?

Has comparison created tension in any of your relationships? If so, how?

I think about the tension Jacob created between himself and Esau. What agony they must have both been in. How much time was wasted. And now the tension Laban created between Rachel and Leah would go on and on.

It's like this circle of chaos getting bigger and bigger each time it goes round.

This was a completely unfair situation Rachel, Leah, and Jacob have found themselves in. What Jacob did to Esau was unfair. What Laban did to Jacob was unfair both to Jacob and to Rachel, and to Leah for that matter. There will always be unfair situations you and I find ourselves in. But we don't have to let life's unfair circumstances cause us to make more poor choices. We can stop the chaotic circle.

Today I want you to work on a combating the chaotic circle comparison strategy. I know, that's a mouthful! But this is to help stop the chaotic circle that keeps trying to engulf us. It will help us get ahead of comparison before it ruins us, and it will lead us to live that life we will be glad to look back on.

The chart provided will help you get started with the process of ending the chaotic comparison circle around you. Fill in each of the blanks. I've provided a few extras for you to craft your own. Figure out how comparison is trying to keep you trapped in that circle, go to God's Word to find your solution, and break out of it.

WHEN COMPARISON MAKES ME BELIEVE I AM ...	I'LL READ ...	AND IT WILL REMIND ME ...
Unheard	1 John 5:14	God _____ me.
Lost	Philippians 1:6	My story isn't _____.
Judged	Romans 8:1	I am not _____.

MID-WEEK TRUTH CHECK-IN

TRUTH TWO:
See it like it really is.

Last week we did a truth check-in on honesty. We allowed ourselves to admit that this struggle of comparison is often one we live in denial about. We dismissed denial and dishonesty, and invited honesty in. But can I tell you something? Even though we accept and know truth, it doesn't mean we always see things for what they really are. As long as we have breath on this earth, we will have an enemy attempting to deceive us.

No, it might not be as extreme as this situation with Jacob, waking up to a wife he didn't realize he married! But, if we're not careful to see this comparison struggle for what it really is, we'll continually be blindsided by it over and over.

READ LUKE 8:17.

What does this verse say will happen to everything that has been concealed?

What are some obstacles that can keep us from seeing things like they really are?

Look up the following verses and fill in the blanks:

PSALM 86:11: We have to ask God to _____ us His truth.

EPHESIANS 4:25: When we know truth, we _____ truth to each other.

PROVERBS 28:18 (NIV): Walking in truth will keep us _____.

On a scale of 1-10, (with 1 being not truthful at all and 10 being always truthful), how would you rate your level of walking in truth as of today?

1   2   3   4   5   6   7   8   9   10

What are at least three things you can do to make sure you're always moving forward with truth?

1.

2.

3.

Sorry Not Sorry

So he said to Laban, "What is this you have done to me?
GENESIS 29:25b

Beginning Prayer:

_____

_____

_____

There's no mistake on this after-wedding morning. Everyone is seeing things as they really are. The lie has been uncovered, and the light is revealing who is whom and what is what.

It doesn't seem like anyone but Laban is winning here. He pulled off the ultimate manipulative maneuver.

> Jacob is about to confront this situation head-on. What three questions does Jacob ask Laban in Genesis 29:25?
>
> 1.
>
> 2.
>
> 3.

These questions don't really feel like questions though, do they? They kind of feel like accusations or *how-dare-yous*. And yes, Jacob has every right to be mad. This isn't what he signed up for. And even though Jacob might be reaping what he sowed for all his trickery, it's still a really awful situation.

There's no denying Laban blatantly planned this wedding. Laban recognized that he had struck gold with Jacob. He was physically strong (remember the episode with the stone over the well), experienced with livestock, and was a captive audience, so to speak.

Laban had Jacob and knew it. He planned and plotted this, though we don't know how early on the scheme began to form in his mind. He realized that he could get another seven years of labor from Jacob, something no one would have been willing to do for Leah, and most likely not even for Rachel. Under normal circumstances, he would have gotten less from another suitor for Rachel and a lot less for Leah. So he cashed in on the situation and got *fourteen* years of skilled labor from a man whom he had over a barrel. Laban held all the cards, and he played them all to his own advantage.

Desperation can do some crazy things to us, can't it?

Let's hear Laban's explanation.

READ GENESIS 29:26-27 AND FILL IN THE BLANKS:

Laban says, "It's not the _____ to give the _____ daughter."

He tells Jacob he must finish the _____ week.

And work another _____ years.

Laban wasn't known as the kindest soul. (Maybe this is why no one wanted to marry into his family.) We will see his fury come out in other ways in the days to come as we continue to study this story. I wonder if Rachel and Leah, out of fear, felt like they had to follow through with his scheming plan. It kind of makes me feel sick when I think about it. My guess is that Rachel was not in on the deception. She would not have wanted to share a husband with her sister.

What are your thoughts about Laban's "explanation"?

At this point, Jacob had lived over seven years in Haran. That's a long time to not know a custom. Especially a custom like this. All those days Jacob was out there working hard for Laban, keeping his eye on the prize, Rachel. So, this "custom" that Laban is now throwing into the mix is just insane. It's not a valid explanation.

We've all experienced some type of deception by someone close to us. We have to be aware. On guard. Ready. All the time. Because deception is everywhere. Which is why our second truth for this combating comparison journey is so incredibly important.

There's an online satire magazine that has confused a lot of people the last few months. My friend Grace is one such person.

She and I were talking about mutual acquaintances in our area who were mentioned in an article that had been swirling around Facebook. She was in shock over the details of this article because it revealed something bad about our mutual acquaintances. Because she was so troubled by this article, I asked her a few more questions about the source.

I quickly realized that Grace had read an article from this satire magazine. I tried to explain to her that news source was fake. They were successful because they made up things just to make fun of people and cause a stir on the Internet.

Grace was shocked. She couldn't believe she had been duped into believing this article. But it happens to the best of us, especially in this virtual world we constantly find ourselves scrolling through. We've all been there, right? Reading things. Looking at pictures. Making assumptions.

Which is why it's so important, now more than ever, to see things for what they really are. The enemy of our souls, Satan, has really pulled a fast one over so many of us. I wonder how many relationships have been broken because of false news flashing before our eyes? In this comparison struggle, there's always what we see, and then there's the unseen. The story behind the story.

So before we compare, we have to ask ourselves, *Is this a story God is writing or is this a story the enemy is writing?*

Laban wrote his own story. Unfortunately, by the time Jacob saw it for what it really was, it was too late. Tomorrow we'll see Jacob's reaction. It's one you won't want to miss.

Whatever It Takes

And Jacob did just that. He finished the week of celebration,
and Laban gave him his daughter Rachel as his wife.
GENESIS 29:28

Beginning Prayer:

_____

_____

_____

When is the last time you decided to do something difficult, no matter what it took? This is where I struggle the most with freedom. I want it, but I'm not always willing to do whatever it takes to get it.

I'm inspired by Jacob's reaction towards Laban. Rather than fighting Laban or doing something dishonorable in retaliation, Genesis 29:28 shows us that Jacob has grown up. His heart seems to have changed since his deceptive days with Isaac and Esau.

This is a very different version of Jacob we're seeing since his fall-out with his brother. That Jacob was a man who would fight fire with fire. This is a much humbler Jacob. He seems to accept the situation for what it is at this point. He knows he's been deceived but is willing to do whatever it takes to get the end result he wants.

It's as if Jacob has learned a valuable lesson. The only person we should strive to be better than is the person we were yesterday. Jacob could have divorced Leah. But he didn't. In this traditional society, divorce was *strongly* disapproved of and would bring significant social stigma. Also, if Jacob had sent Leah away, Laban would probably have been able to take Rachel back as well.

We don't know all the thoughts behind every action. We do know that Jacob accepted the situation, but he didn't settle.

How long does verse 28 say it was before Jacob was able to have Rachel as his wife?

A. One year

B. One week

C. Seven years

D. One month

In Jacob's heart, it didn't really matter how much time had to pass. Because every moment felt like an eternity while he was waiting for this woman he adored. But what were those moments like for Leah? And what were they like for Rachel?

When the week was finished, Laban came through on his word. Jacob and Rachel were finally able to say, "I do."

There were also two other ladies entering this story.

Read Genesis 29:24. Who came with Leah?

Read Genesis 29:29. Who came with Rachel?

A few months ago, I started getting sucked into a show called *Downton Abby*. It took me a little while to get into it, but once I did, I couldn't stop watching. In fact, I may or may not have spent half a day one Sunday watching an entire season. But I had to stop because book deadlines mean you have to control yourself.

Ahem.

If you're not familiar with the show, *Downton Abby* chronicles the lives wealthy and influential British family. One of the things I was most fascinated about was watching each the ladies of the estate interact with their lady's maid. These maids did everything for their ladies. Picked out their clothes. Helped them get dressed. Made sure they were where they were supposed to be. Did all their cleaning. Laundry. Grooming. I mean, everything.

Every once in a while, especially during busy travel seasons, I make room in our budget to have someone help me with some cleaning. It's quite glorious to walk into a bathroom that is clean, and I didn't have to clean it.

But honestly, I can't imagine what it would be like to have someone waiting on me hand and foot all day long. It sounds nice—for a few minutes. But I kinda like my space. I don't know that I would be OK with having someone that close to my personal business. All. Day. Long.

FUN FACT:
According to
wedding customs
mentioned in
the Bible the
bridal week
was seven days
of celebration.[21]

Zilpah and Bilhah were to serve Rachel and Leah in a way similar to the *Downton Abby* lady's maids. Maybe it sounds nice, but as we continue to look at this story through a lens of truth, seeing it like it really was, it might not have been as nice as it sounded.

Be honest, would you want someone to wait on you hand and foot all day every day? No judgment zone here!
Yes or No? Explain.

What do you think might have been some potential problems with having someone so close to you in this situation?

What would be some of the benefits?

We're almost ready to wrap up this week of our study. I don't like leaving you on the note I'm about to leave you on, but there's one last point we need to see this week.

READ GENESIS 29:30.

What does this verse say about Jacob's feelings toward Rachel?

This story is making my head spin. We've already seen several examples of how comparison is creating tension. List at least three examples of comparison we've studied so far:

1.

2.

3.

There are two ways we could take this ending of our study this week.

One, we could justify Jacob's feelings and say, "Oh well, he never really liked Leah in the first place." Or, we could say, "That's so messed up Jacob, you should love them both equally." But he didn't. His heart was clearly pointed toward Rachel.

How do you think this made Leah feel?

The reality is, if we base our worth on the value others place on us, we'll always be disappointed. There's always going to be someone to whom we don't measure up, and people in our lives who point out our failures every chance they get.

But God does whatever it takes for us to believe that we are His pick. His choice. That's made clear through the cross. You are the one He wants to use, to call out of this generation, and to raise up to do great things for His name.

As we wrap up this week, I want you to spend some time getting even more honest with God. Ask Him to allow you to see this struggle for what it really is in your life. I've got some questions for you to answer. Take your time, journal, and process this with God.

Do you believe God looks at you less than someone else?
Yes or No? Explain.

Tell God about the last time you felt like you didn't measure up.

Are you living the life you've always hoped for? Yes or No?
Explain.

Tell God what you're still longing for:

Has God revealed things to you this week that maybe you weren't seeing like they really were? Yes or No? Explain.

If yes, ask God to help you know what you need to do with the truth you've seen. If no, ask God to show you, right now, if there's anything you're not seeing like it really is.

You Be You

What is your comparison zone?

1. When another girl walks in the room, you are most likely to notice:
    A. Her physical appearance
    B. How expensive her purse or shoes are
    C. If she has a boyfriend or friends with her
    D. What she is talking about

2. The articles you read online, mainly discuss:
    A. Celebrity relationship updates
    B. How to prepare for college or a career
    C. Tips for eating healthy
    D. How to improve your grades

3. On Pinterest®, you like to pin:
    A. You don't really pin, you'd rather be on Twitter
    B. OOTD and new workout routines
    C. Forget Pinterest, I'd rather make a wish list on Amazon
    D. Movie quotes about love

4. Reoccurring words in my prayers are:
    A. Money, allowance, need
    B. Someone, heart, alone
    C. Plans, school, practice
    D. Self-control, perseverance, weight

5. You often feel intimidated if another girl has:
    A. Better grades than you
    B. A smaller jean size
    C. Nicer clothes
    D. More friends than you

RESULTS:

Question 1	Question 2	Question 3	Question 4	Question 5
A) 1	A) 3	A) 4	A) 2	A) 4
B) 2	B) 4	B) 1	B) 3	B) 1
C) 3	C) 1	C) 2	C) 4	C) 2
D) 4	D) 2	D) 3	D) 1	D) 3

Mostly 1s

You tend to compare yourself to others in the realm of Physical Appearance.

Mostly 2s

You tend to compare yourself to others in the realm of Money or Wealth.

Mostly 3s

You tend to compare in the realm of Relationships.

Mostly 4s

You tend to compare in the realm of School or Academics.

Week
Three

TRUTH THREE:

You don't always have to be OK.

COMBATING COMPARISON VERSE THREE:
*This is the confidence we have in approaching
God: that if we ask anything according
to his will, he hears us.*
1 JOHN 5:14 (NIV)

Warm Things Up

Here are a few questions to get your group talking!

What are some things you learned from this week's personal study?

How did comparison show up in your life this week?

Do you have a chaotic comparison cycle going on in your life? Explain. How are you doing at stopping this cycle?

Are you walking in truth and moving forward in truth? Explain. What seems to be your biggest hindrance?

Watch

To hear more from Nicki, download the optional video bundle to view the Week Three teaching at www.LifeWay.com/RachelandLeah.

Create Conversation

Its _____ to not be _____ sometimes, but it's not _____ to never be not _____.

What really important question did Nicki say we should ask ourselves and each other? Why is this a better question to ask than "How are you?"

What does 1 John 5:14 mean? What does it not mean?

Why is it important to honestly admit to ourselves and others when we are not OK?

What is wrong with remaining not OK? How can we help each other when things are not OK?

Have a "soul check" to close your session. Lead girls to pair up and ask each other "How's your soul?" Encourage honest conversation, then direct them to pray for each other.

It'll Be OK, Just Not Today

When the LORD saw that Leah was unloved, He opened
her womb; but Rachel was unable to conceive.
GENESIS 29:31

Beginning Prayer:
Before you begin each study,
jot down a personal prayer here.

_____

_____

_____

As I'm typing these words, I'm living through one of the hardest seasons I've ever experienced. A few months ago my mom was in a horrible car accident that forced her to get an MRI to search for broken bones. The test revealed something more horrible than any broken bone: a large brain tumor.

I could probably write an entire book on the suffering this season has brought. I wouldn't wish it on anyone. Brain tumors do horrific things to people, making them become someone they aren't. It's a slow, painful death. This season has stretched me beyond my capacity.

You know that proverbial but non-biblical phrase: God never gives you more than you can handle?

Out. The. Window.

I've gotten so tired of people telling me it's going to be OK. There's never been a day during this season when I've walked out of my mom's room, whether in the hospital, rehab, or nursing home, and thought, "It's going to be OK."

The reality is, it will be OK. Just not today. Or tomorrow, or probably the next day.

My heart aches when people say things like *what doesn't kill you makes you stronger*. While that may be true, the reality is what doesn't kill you still hurts.

One day, yes, God will right all the wrongs in this world. Sin will be no more. Darkness will forever flee. You and I will be completely healed and whole. But until that day comes, there's going to be some not-so-OK days.

And it's OK to say, "I'm not OK." In fact, that's our third truth:

You don't always have to be OK.

The problem comes when these not-OK days just keep stacking up. And the life that once looked so hopeful now seems so gloomy. We have to find a way to admit our suffering and find sanity in the midst of it.

The reality is not every story in our lives or in the Bible ends with everyone living happily ever after. Rachel's and Leah's story isn't one that we'll be able to wrap a pretty little bow around. It's messy from start to finish. And this week's reading is no different.

READ GENESIS 29:30-35.

What does verse 30 say about the way Jacob felt toward Rachel?

How might a statement like that have impacted Leah?

Fill in the blanks for verse 31(a):
When the Lord _____ _____ Leah was _____,
he _____ her _____.

This is where things go from messy to messier between these two sisters. They've gone from being sisters to rivals. Because what does verse 31b say about Rachel?

She was _____ to conceive.

Let's go back to a very important word in today's study.

I've tried not to give you the answers because hey, this is your study. But, the word you wrote in the first blank on verse 31 should have been *saw*. This isn't just something to breeze over. Do we really take the time to comprehend what it means to know that God sees our moments of suffering?

How does Colossians 1:15 describe Jesus?

What does 2 Corinthians 5:7 say we walk by?

Write out Hebrews 4:13:

If nothing is hidden from the invisible God, then we have to trust that every ache we experience He sees. And if He saw Leah's pain, He is also seeing mine and yours.

Sometimes it's enough to know God sees. Sometimes it's not.

But when God sees, He takes the action He sees fit. For Leah, He saw the best thing was to open her womb, to give her a baby. Sounds sweet, right? Leah's unloved and so it seems like God is blessing her with a child.

That's how we can rationalize what God is doing and attempt to make sense of this situation.

God also sees my pain. And He knows how much I want my mom to be healed here on this earth. But He's not healing her. She's dying.

I could give you some Christianized phrase like, "Oh God's healing her, it will just be in heaven." But no. That's not what I've been asking for.

Leah didn't ask for a baby. She desired love from Jacob. Something she just couldn't seem to gain. Instead of love, she got a baby. Ironically, that was Rachel's greatest desire.

Faith does not mean that everything is going to turn out OK. Faith means we trust God even when things aren't OK.

TURN TO ROMANS 8:38-39.

What, according to these two verses, cannot separate you from the love of God? Make a list, and next to each item write what this might correspond to in your life today:

As I'm thinking about the season I'm in right now, I've had to fully admit: I'm not OK. I scroll through social media and see everyone living their lives as usual. But while everyone is moving forward, I just seem to be standing still in this place of not being OK, day after day.

As I'm reading Romans 8:38-39 and thinking of Leah, this woman so unloved by man but so loved by God, something is settling deep in my heart.

Whether our pain is inflicted by others or not, life will leave all of us feeling unloved at some point or another. We will experience a loss or grieve in a way that makes us feel like we're missing out as the world continues spinning.

But our souls can rest in this place of believing that no matter what happens, no matter how many un-OK days we live out, there is nothing that can keep us from the individual, unique love God has for each of us.

NOTHING. NO-THING. No thing. No man. No issue. No struggle. No fear. No uncertainty. No, nothing.

What is that thing in your life right now that's making you feel not OK?

What do you think comparison will do to that struggle if you don't bring it under the love of God?

I can tell you from my own experience right now, that the days I don't consciously meditate on the love of God, comparison shows its ugly head in so many ways.

When I'm scrolling through social media and I see my friends out to lunch or on coffee dates, I'm asking, "Why Lord?" Or when my kids need me to be at one of their events but I can't, yet I see all the other moms who can, I ask ,"Why Lord?" And the list could go on and on.

When do you find yourself asking, "Why Lord?"

On the days I bring this battle under the love of God, there's a whole lot less scrolling through social media. I'm able to see each day as a gift—something to treasure.

So it's OK to not be OK. It's OK to say we're not OK. But one day it will be OK. And until it's OK again, God promises nothing will keep us from His love for us. Nothing.

This is what this feels like.

Leah conceived, gave birth to a son, and named him Reuben, for she said,
"The Lord has seen my affliction, surely my husband will love me now."
GENESIS 29:32

Beginning Prayer:

_____

_____

_____

In the midst of this difficult season, my three daughters have been over-the-top amazing. They've traded the fun days of summer for sitting beside a hospital bed.

On the last day of summer, I knew I needed to do something special for my girls. The problem was, no one could agree on what was considered fun. I ended up sending the oldest two off with a paid tank of gas so they could have their own outdoor adventure. Then my husband and I took our youngest daughter to a local amusement park.

When you only have three people at an amusement park, one person has to ride solo. So we took turns. Eventually it was my turn to ride alone.

We waited patiently in line and then climbed aboard our coaster train.

As the ride started, for some reason I got so teary. Grief has this way of just popping up out of nowhere. As cheesy as this sounds, it was as if this roller coaster was the perfect real-life picture of what the last few months had felt like.

At first, like at the coaster station, you start off with a lot of people beside you. But then, they fade and you find yourself alone, going through these up and down motions. Twists and turns. Sudden stops. Sudden starts. Ultimately you end up in the same spot you started.

And the next day it begins all over again.

It doesn't have to be a tragedy or crisis that brings these types of emotions. Any type of affliction to our souls has the potential to make us feel this way.

Unloved Leah reaches a place in her life where she believes God sees her pain. But is that enough? To just know that He sees? Let's find out.

READ GENESIS 29:30-32.

What did Leah name her first son? Circle the correct answer.

Adam   Jacob   Isaac   Laban   Reuben   Samuel

Why did she give him this name (v. 32)?

How did she hope this baby would change her relationship with Jacob?

We're about to see a pattern with Leah and these babies—a pattern I think all of us could admit to experiencing at one point or another in our lives.

Comparison convinces us that if God did something for someone else, He should do the same for us. This is a dangerous place for a girl's soul to rest. I would love to tell you that just because God did it for her, God will do the same for you. But I've learned painfully through this season of affliction that this isn't always the case. However, that doesn't mean that what God has for us isn't beautiful and just what we need.

According to dictionary.com, the word *affliction* means:

Something that causes pain or suffering.[1]

I can find no verse in the Bible that tells me there will be no pain or suffering in this life. In fact, I find the opposite. There are dozens of verses that remind me that when affliction comes, God is close. In fact, my friend, I can guarantee you will have affliction in your life. Not just once. Or twice. Many times.

But God is writing something special through our affliction journeys. Just because your story doesn't look like *hers* and it's painful, doesn't mean there's not something good unfolding.

Perhaps that's what Leah is sharing with us as she says, "The Lord has seen my affliction" (v. 32). She knows that God sees. Unfortunately, she's hoping God's blessing is the means to end her pain of not having Jacob's love. The blessing of the child and God's care for her are not enough. She's willing to say or do whatever it takes to gain the one thing her heart longs for.

We joke about having things like retail therapy or eating chocolate. But when we're experiencing affliction, we just want something or someone to make us feel better.

There's nothing more I want for my mom than to see her healed right now. I would love to walk into her hospice room later today and find her completely whole. I've seen God do that for other people—just heal them in an instant.

But the reality is, I don't know that my mom will be healed. By the time you hold these words in your hands, I'll know the answer. And we don't know if Jacob ever really loved Leah.

> When was the last time you hoped God would fix a problem or struggle in your life? What happened?

What will Leah do with this pain? What will I do with my pain? What will you do with your pain? And what will we do in the future with the pain that is still to come? These are the questions we must wrestle with in order to live out the unique purpose God has given us. I know it sounds so typical, but there's a purpose in our pain. And until we admit we're not OK, God can't do much with us or for us.

Leah is admitting she's not OK. But because of what she's asking God to do through her pain, we see that her theology is a bit off. This is where it's so important to understand that just because the Bible reports someone saying something about God, doesn't mean their words reflect the true character of God.

Here's what I mean. Most of the stories in the Bible offer us one of two ways to learn:

Descriptive or Prescriptive

These are fancy terms. You and I probably don't talk like this. If you do, awesome. But I don't. However, it's really important to know the difference between these two types of scriptural texts when we're studying.

Descriptive texts are used by the author to simply inform us of what happened. Yes, there's always something to learn and apply from these types of texts. A great example of a descriptive book of the Bible is Judges.

What is an example of a descriptive text you've read before?

Prescriptive texts are used by the author to instruct us on how to live the way God hopes for us to live. The Ten Commandments, the Book of Proverbs, and Paul's letters are all great examples of prescriptive texts.

What is an example of a prescriptive text you've read before?

If I were going to re-label these, I would call them *Know This* (descriptive) and *Do This* (prescriptive).

We're studying a descriptive text. Just because Leah says the reason God is giving her a baby is because of the pain she's feeling, doesn't mean it is. It could be. Or it could be because God is unfolding a greater purpose through her pain.

Sometimes the greatest *no* we hear from God unfolds into the greatest *yes* our lives could experience. We will see something beautiful unfold through Leah and Rachel. But it's wrapped in so many comparison, competition, and control issues.

As we continue to study this descriptive text, we will see truth and learn lessons from Leah's and Rachel's story. As we wrap up today's study, I want you to list the lessons you've learned so far. We've still got a ways to go and much to learn, but what has God revealed to you so far?

Write it out here:

_____

_____

_____

_____

_____

_____

_____

_____

_____

_____

_____

_____

_____

_____

_____

_____

_____

_____

TRUTH THREE:
You don't always have to be OK.

This week the truth we're telling ourselves is: *You don't always have to be OK*. Being honest before God not only about where we are but also about where we want to be is incredibly powerful. He never rejects any of our questions, wonderings, or doubts.

> Turn back to the first page of this week and fill in the blanks for this week's Combating Comparison Verse.

> This is the _____ we have in _____ God: that if we ask anything _____ to his will, _____ _____ us
> 1 John 5:14 (NIV).

Remember yesterday when we learned about prescriptive texts? This is one of those. There's a do-this answer to our God-struggles. But we have to know and believe the truth of this verse in order for it to soothe the places that aren't making a lot of sense.

Prayer is not something we do in order to get something we want. We can't bring our list of demands and expect God to deliver. Prayer is the most humble, highest, and honorable place we can go with God.

But we over-complicate it. I know, as a woman who struggles with comparison, I sometimes wonder, "Does God even want to hear my prayers? Her's are so much better."

My friend Wendy Pope has one of the best quotes on prayer I've ever heard. She said, "I'm not an expert on prayer, I'm just a woman who prays."

I love that so much. God isn't looking for prayer experts. He's looking for people who will just pray.

> What do you think it means when the verse says to pray "according to His will"?

Turn to John 15:7. What does it look like for you personally to abide/remain in Jesus?

So when we're not feeling OK, it's OK. But there has to come a point when we start to shift. Satan would love for us to settle in that state of not being OK, where day after day we stay wrapped up in our sorrow and affliction.

When we pray we become more and more like Jesus and less and less like anyone else.

There's no right or wrong way to pray. But I want to leave you with these three S's. They help me when I'm not sure how to pray, in those times when I'm not feeling OK.

1. Start.

Just start talking. Lay it all out before God. He can handle it all. The tears. The fears. The doubts. The frustrations. Tell Him everything. Hold nothing back.

2. Scripture.

Pray God's Word over the situation. This is such a powerful thing to do when we don't know what to pray. If you're not sure where to begin, use the Combating Comparison Verses throughout this study. They are a fabulous place to start. Just read the Scripture and declare the truth over your situation. I find reading God's Word aloud when I'm praying is a very powerful thing to do as well.

3. Surrender.

This is the biggie. When we're not feeling OK, typically it's because there's something we need to surrender to God in our lives. For Leah, it was Jacob's love. For me, right now it's believing God is still good, even if He doesn't heal my mom. For you, it could be a dozen things—a friendship, a possession, or a life situation. Whatever it is, be willing to surrender the thing that's making you feel like you are not OK.

You may have to repeat this prayer process several times before your soul starts to feel OK again. But I promise, if you'll keep bringing it to God, as our verse this weeks says, He hears you.

Her Three Sons

She conceived again, gave birth to a son, and said,
"The LORD heard that I am unloved and has given
me this son also." So she named him Simeon.

GENESIS 29:33

Beginning Prayer:

_____

_____

_____

When a girl's soul is tired, there is no amount of sleep that can fix it.

I love to people watch. A few days ago I found myself at a busy park. America, we just look tired. It's all over our faces. Our bodies are crying out. And listen, I'm leading the pack in this. I'm no exception.

But I'm seeing the results of this roller coaster of comparison. It's wearing us out. Making us more tired than we've ever been. And it's creating a spirit of striving that we have to stop.

It's making us "not OK."

I'm not saying we should just pack it all up and Netflix® binge until the end of time. We've got work to do. Assignments to complete. We need to equip ourselves to complete this God-given desire.

If we just quit everything, we'll be miserable and broke. God designed us to work. Immediately after Adam and Eve were created, they had stuff to do (Gen. 2:15).

I'm not just talking about being busy-tired. I'm talking about a soul-struggle. Leah experienced this. She kept doing the same thing over and over. Her constant striving to obtain Jacob's love had to make her soul weary. It was a chase that led her to the same starting position over and over.

READ GENESIS 29:33.

What did Leah name her second son?

What does this verse say about the way she felt after her second son was born?

READ GENESIS 29:34.

What did Leah name her third son?

What were her hopes for her relationship with Jacob now?

Three sons and still no love from Jacob. The heartache Leah felt was real. There's no getting around it. She had to face this disappointment day after day.

Leah is on what I call a "maybe-now" journey.

Baby One: Maybe now Jacob will love me.

Baby Two: Maybe now Jacob will love me.

Baby Three: Maybe *now* Jacob will love me.

If we're going to be honest about this comparison struggle, I think each of us could admit to some type of *maybe now* search in our own lives. People can be mean and cruel without even intentionally doing it. Sometimes, without even saying a word, they make us feel less than, as though we don't measure up and aren't good enough.

Maybe Jacob was treating Leah in such a way to make her feel like striving was her only option.

The more we define success by how other people see us, the more we will strive to be successful in their eyes. *Maybe nows* convince us there's more to do, say, or become in order to have that longing fulfilled.

What is an example of a *maybe now* you have chased in your life?

How does chasing a *maybe now* leave us in a place of comparison?

How do we find holy honesty and confidence without comparison wrapped into one package? And have quick access to it so that we can access it at just the right time and allow God's love to cover every ounce of affliction in our lives?

Well, I think tomorrow we will see something Leah did to shift her mentality on this struggle. It helped her find the strength to be okay again. And I really believe it will help you and me if we'll press into this process.

As we wrap up today's study, I want us to reflect a little bit on how things were going for Rachel at this point.

Go back and read Genesis 29:31. How many children did Rachel have at this point?
A. Two
B. Zero
C. One

Why do you think it was significant for the author to tell us this detail about Rachel?

How could this detail have created tension between Rachel and Leah?

We're gonna see things get really ugly between these sisters. But before we go there, let's see what Leah does after she gives birth to her fourth baby. See you on the next page!

But This Time

And she conceived again, gave birth to a son, and said,
"This time I will praise the Lord." Therefore she named
him Judah. Then Leah stopped having children.
GENESIS 29:35

Beginning Prayer:

_____

_____

_____

Would you say you're a fast or slow learner?

Sometimes I wonder how many times I have to go around a mountain before I conquer it. It often feels like *so many times*.

Leah has gone around the *maybe-now* mountain three times. Let's see what happens in our study today.

So far Leah has given birth to three sons. Each of their names signified something about how Leah felt at the time they were born.

Son One: Reuben

Leah conceived, gave birth to a son, and named him Reuben, for she said,
"The LORD has seen my affliction; surely now my husband will love me."
GENESIS 29:32

His name in Hebrew meant, "Behold a son!"[2] There was a hope in his birth for Leah, a hope that perhaps this would be the bridge between her and Jacob.

Son Two: Simeon

> She conceived again, gave birth to a son, and said, "The LORD heard that I am unloved and has given me this son also." So she named him Simeon.
> GENESIS 29:33

His name came from the Hebrew word *shama*[3] which means, "to hear."[4]

Son Three: Levi

> She conceived again, gave birth to a son, and said, "At last, my husband will become attached to me because I have borne three sons for him." Therefore he was named Levi.
> GENESIS 29:34

There's a little uncertainty around Levi's name origin. But some people believe it meant "joined or attached"[5] in Hebrew, which would definitely make sense considering what Leah said.

READ GENESIS 29:35.

What did Leah name her fourth son?

Fill in the blanks for Leah's statement after he was born:
This _____ I will _____ the _____.

It's not totally clear why Leah shifts her tone here. Perhaps she's accepted the fact that Jacob isn't going to love her no matter what. Maybe it's that she's so grateful for this baby boy. Or it could be that she is just overwhelmed with God's goodness.

We've seen a pattern with the other baby names. They all reflected something happening deep inside her. The name *Judah* means "praise"[6] and the word *Jew* is a shortened form of "Judah."[7]

What are some typical reactions we have when things aren't going the way we hoped? Try to think of at least three.

1.

2.

3.

When I was thinking that last question through, I can assure you I didn't think of the word *praise*. It doesn't tend to be our go-to reaction toward affliction. Most of the time when we're going around and around the same mountain there's a lot of grumbling, complaining, and a lot of that "Why Me?!" question.

Whatever it is that has changed inside of Leah, it's like she's OK again. Her soul has found rest. She's at peace with the situation. At least for now.

What will it take for you and me to be able to shift our attitude to a place of praise?

TURN TO ISAIAH 43:21.

What does this verse say the people God formed will do?

God is speaking through the prophet Isaiah in this verse. He's reminding us that praise is a huge part of who we are as children of God. It's not because God is some ego-driven being who needs us to high-five Him all day long. It's way beyond anything like that.

> **FAST FACT:**
> Isaiah actually descended through Leah.[8]

READ 1 PETER 2:9. FILL IN THE BLANKS.

God says:
We are a royal _____.

A _____ nation.

People for His _____.

And all of this is so that we will _____ the
_____ of the One who _____ us out of
_____ and into _____.

What does Genesis 29:35 say happened to Leah after her fourth baby was born?

It seems like Leah has accepted what's what. And it seems like she's moving forward. But as we'll see next week, she really hasn't. She's looking over her shoulder, seeing what Rachel's up to, watching her and Jacob. Something is stirring deeper than we could ever imagine.

But for today, we celebrate Leah's moment of praise.

> How does shifting our perspective toward praise help us accept our situations and not compare our circumstances with others?

As we wrap up our study for this week, I want us to step into a place of praise. Listen friend, I get it. My heart's desires are not fulfilled right now either. I want to see my mom healed and whole. I want this nightmare to be over and life to be normal again.

But like Leah, I'm accepting things for what they are. I know that my God has created me with a holy endurance, and I will call forth that endurance by being able to shift and praise.

Below is something I've been praying during these difficult days. I'm sharing these vulnerable words with you today not for your sympathy but to help us both. At end of this prayer there's a place for you to write a "this time" prayer of praise.

This Time Prayer

> God, You've seen my efforts, You've counted my tears, and You've nudged me toward perseverance. You've heard the prayers I've prayed and the words I've spoken, both tender and harsh. I've asked You again and again for this one thing. But this one thing You have not granted. And so today, I surrender it fully into Your hands. I will not chase any more maybe nows, and I will stand firm knowing that even when You don't do what my heart desires, You are still a good God.
>
> So,
>
> This time instead of weeping, I will worship.
>
> This time instead of over-thinking, I will proclaim your goodness to someone.

This time instead of questioning Your sovereignty, I will surrender my secret places.

This time instead of doubting my worth, I will find value in Your promises for my life.

This time instead of grumbling, I will be grateful.

Write your own:

This time, instead of _____, I will _____.

_____

_____

_____

_____

_____

_____

_____

_____

_____

_____

_____

_____

_____

_____

_____

_____

You Be You

What is your Sunday style?

1. Your Sunday afternoon is best described as:
   - A. Productive
   - B. Conversational
   - C. Restful
   - D. Fun

2. By Sunday night, you feel:
   - A. Like you've connected with your friends
   - B. Like you've seen or done something enjoyable
   - C. Like you're ready for the upcoming week
   - D. Like you wish your sweatpants could be worn on Monday too

3. Your Sunday sticky notes include:
   - A. Tasks to accomplish
   - B. Chores, homework assignments, and movie times
   - C. What sticky notes? Where's my pillow?
   - D. Prayer requests you didn't want to forget

4. If you miss your Sunday routine you feel:
   - A. Like a good time passed you by
   - B. A little cranky or weary
   - C. Behind and not ready for Monday
   - D. Like you missed out on fellowship

5. You smile when you think about:
   - A. The fun you had on Sunday
   - B. The slow pace of Sunday
   - C. The stories that were shared on Sunday
   - D. The work accomplished on Sunday

RESULTS:

Question 1	Question 2	Question 3	Question 4	Question 5
A) 1	A) 2	A) 1	A) 4	A) 4
B) 2	B) 4	B) 4	B) 3	B) 3
C) 3	C) 1	C) 3	C) 1	C) 2
D) 4	D) 3	D) 2	D) 2	D) 1

Mostly 1s

Your Sunday style is: Pretty Prepared

Your outfit for tomorrow is laid out and your homework is complete. Sunday is for getting things done and keeping things in order. Monday will not catch you by surprise.

Mostly 2s

Your Sunday style is: Fabulously Friendly

Whether you have people over at your house or go out with your friends, Sunday is for fellowship and making connections.

Mostly 3s

Your Sunday style is: Refreshingly Rejuvenated

Blankets, leggings, and Netflix oh my! Whether you are sleeping or just enjoying some downtime. Sunday is your time to unwind and rest.

Mostly 4s

Your Sunday style is: The Glorious Go-Getter

You want to get in the car and go. You might take a hike, go fishing, see a movie, or go bowling, but weekends were made for activity! It's a #SundayFunday.

Week
four

TRUTH FOUR:

You didn't do anything wrong.

COMBATING COMPARISON VERSE FOUR:
*A person's heart plans his way,
but the Lᴏʀᴅ determines his steps.*
PROVERBS 16:9

Warm Things Up

Here are a few questions to get your group talking!

What are some things you learned from this week's personal study?

How did comparison show up in your life this week?

What's the difference between a *descriptive* and *prescriptive* text? Give an example of each.

What *maybe now* journey have you been on lately? How has this affected the comparison battle in your life?

How have you applied the Combating Comparison Verse this week?

Watch

To hear more from Nicki, download the optional video bundle to view the Week Four teaching at www.LifeWay.com/RachelandLeah.

Create Conversation

When life doesn't turn out as you hope it will, do you blame yourself? If yes, why? If not, who do you blame?

Is it comforting to know that sometimes, "You didn't do anything wrong"?

When things don't go the way that you've hoped, do you run *to* God or *from* God? What needs to change for you to run to God?

Does the saying "busyness is effectiveness" resonate with you? Explain. What does God's definition of success look like?

Name practical ways you can serve others by making them feel valued and welcomed, as God has welcomed you.

Close by praying the girls in your group will feel the freedom to run to God with their struggles and disappointments.

Soul Dysfunction

When Rachel saw that she was not bearing Jacob any children, she
envied her sister. "Give me sons, or I will die!" she said to Jacob.
GENESIS 30:1

Beginning Prayer:
Before you begin each study,
jot down a personal prayer here.

Have you ever heard the phrase: "Our family puts the *fun* in dysfunctional"?
I'm pretty sure the Koziarz crew could probably have that phrase put on a
sign and placed at our front door. I like to think we are normal, but we're
not. I mean for goodness' sake, we have livestock as pets. That alone
brings a form of dysfunction I could have never predicted.

But every once in a while I try to keep things a little sane around our house.

So when there is a lot of tension that needs to be talked through, my husband and I will
sometimes call a family meeting. Basically, the whole family is called into the living
room, and we present the issues. At one meeting, Kris, my husband, even pulled out the
ice cream scooper and used it as a gavel to call the meeting to order. Our girls were less
than amused.

I have the *best* intentions with these meetings. They're supposed to be a place everyone
can share what we need to say, and resolve issues. Before I call the meeting, I always have
this picture in my head that we'll all end up hugging and singing Kumbaya.

Lord have mercy, there has never been a family meeting in the Koziarz household that
hasn't ended in tears, screaming, slamming doors, and a thousand more issues brought up
that I never even knew about. Someone is always mad. Something is always unfair. And

there is always someone who needs to go somewhere after the meeting, so could we please hurry up?

Sigh.

I'm sure you have your own brand of dysfunction in your life too. Most of us do. We all have *that* family member. Or *that* weird situation. There's hardly such a thing as a normal family. But as dysfunctional as we seem to be a lot of days, it hardly compares to the dysfunction we're about to uncover in our story this week.

It's about to go up a level of craziness.

READ GENESIS 30:1-7.

What did Rachel say would happen to her if she didn't have a baby? Circle the right answer:

A. She would cry.

B. She would be angry.

C. She would die.

D. She would run away.

Why do you think Rachel was so desperate for a baby?

How did comparison play a role in her sorrow?

Jacob is super honest with Rachel. He's probably just as frustrated as she is. One thing I've come to know about men through my husband, Kris, is they like to fix things. Men tend to naturally head in that direction. We've had to go through numerous struggles, marriage counselors, and pastors to arrive at the place where he understands that sometimes I don't need him to fix anything. I just need him to listen.

Jacob is listening, but he's also fixing. He says in verse 2:

"Am I in God's place, who has withheld offspring from you?"

The reality is both of them needed someone to blame. Rachel is blaming Jacob. Jacob is blaming God. Neither response is really beneficial in a situation like this.

But isn't that our natural tendency as humans? When something isn't working, we need someone to blame.

It's one of the reasons our family meetings end up being so incredibly dysfunctional. Someone wants to blame someone for something, and no one wants to own their issues.

The Bible doesn't tell us how long Rachel and Jacob had been trying to have a baby. But we can know that those two desperate statements from both of them came from a deep struggle.

Rachel's comparison with her sister was ruining her. It was making her feel less than. She wasn't sure she'd keep measuring up in Jacob's eyes. Rachel needed someone to look at her and say our fourth truth this week:

You didn't do anything wrong.

GO BACK TO GENESIS 29:31.

What does this verse say about Rachel?

Did it say why? No.

Sometimes life throws us a curveball that wasn't necessarily thrown by the hand of God. Life can be filled with unfair, unequal moments. One of the lies comparison tries to make us believe is that we did something wrong that's caused us not to have the one thing we want so badly.

What did Rachel do since she couldn't have a child (v. 4)?

It might be hard for you to understand Rachel's frustration, but in ancient Jewish culture, the inability to have children was considered a sign of God's judgment. Rachel wanted a child more than anything and felt less than because she couldn't conceive.

You might not have wanted a baby, but there's been something in each of our hearts we've so greatly desired. And we've prayed and prayed. Yet each day there's more and more sorrow. Then it crushes us to watch someone else receive what we desire most, again and again and again.

That creates some soul dysfunction in us too.

Here's something I've come to understand about sorrow: While there are times we go through sorrow without it being caused by something we've done, we don't have to conform to it. Sorrow that comes from seeds of comparison hurts. There's no denying it. But there's a place we can turn when we're hurting and want to blame someone or something for what we're feeling.

God's Word

I know this sounds very Christian-Girl of me to say, but I don't just mean open up the Bible and slap a Bible verse Band-Aid on your soul. I mean, go to the Bible to get your strength to keep going—to find the strength to wake up and face tomorrow. Even if that comparison sorrow is still going to be there the next day, and the next day, and the next. But we don't have to let it ruin who we are becoming and what God wants to do in us.

TURN TO PSALM 119:28.

What does this verse say will strengthen us when our souls are weary?

TURN TO PSALM 22:19.

What does this verse teach us to pray when we feel weak?

The challenge and task is to actually believe these truths will work when we don't feel like we're measuring up to the girls around us who seem to have what we want the most.

But taking things into our own hands is risky for a girl who is trying to find her freedom in Jesus. Rachel has taken this situation into her own hands. She sends in her servant to Jacob.

What emotional struggles might Rachel have experienced from encouraging her servant to sleep with Jacob so that she can have this one thing her heart wants?

What does Genesis 30:5 say the baby is?

    A. Boy

    B. Girl

Let's see what other type of soul dysfunction is popping into Rachel's heart.

READ GENESIS 30:6 AND FILL IN THE BLANKS:

Rachel said, "_____ has _____ me; yes, he has _____ me and _____ me a son," so she named him Dan.

Now head to dictionary.com or another dictionary, and look up what the word *vindicated* means. Write the definition:

Remember how we learned that just because someone in the Bible says something about God doesn't mean those words truly reflects God's character or reasoning? We have no proof that this is what God is doing for Rachel. It's an assumption she's making.

Assumptions are something we have to be really careful of making. I'll explain more tomorrow. See you then!

There's a Winner

Rachel said, "In my wrestlings with God, I have wrestled with
my sister and won," and she named him Naphtali.
GENESIS 30:8

Beginning Prayer:

_____

_____

_____

Do you like to play board games?

If I'm going to be honest, I'm not really a fan of them. Mostly because the friends who ask me to play games with them are so incredibly competitive. They like to win. In fact, they will go to extreme measures to win. Cheating. Lying. Laughing until we're crying about the cheating and the lying.

It's funny, but then it's not. You know? I mean, I've seen people straight up leave the table because they were so mad they lost.

Everyone likes to win. And the world tells us there's a winning formula for our lives.

Work hard + Do whatever you have to do + Be the best + Work even harder = Winning

Yesterday we saw Rachel doing whatever she had to do to feel like she could stay in this baby battle. But it didn't stop with one baby.

What does Genesis 30:8 say Rachel named the second baby?

Why did she name him that?

What do you think Rachel meant in her reasoning about his name?

Is it possible that Rachel felt like she had the whole package now? The husband. His love. The servants. And now, the babies.

It is one thing to be jealous of someone for having something you desire. But it is a completely different thing to take matters into your own hands, then stand to proclaim you are somehow the winner of an envy-filled situation.

This isn't a board game gone wrong. This is a serious envy-jealousy battle.

Envy has been the culprit of these internal turned external battles for women since the beginning of time. It's so sad, but so true. We'll get more into this during week six of our study, but other people's winning does not make us losers or vice-versa.

The belief that somehow God doesn't have good things just for us can become a heartbreaking part of our envy. Envy makes us look at everything and everyone around us. Then envy can, like it did with Rachel, cause us to start crafting some not-so-good thoughts.

Thoughts that lead us to say things like we saw Rachel say yesterday:

> Rachel said, "God has vindicated me; yes, he has heard
> me and given me a son," so she named him Dan.
> GENESIS 30:6

There are so many roots of comparison. I believe envy is one of the hardest to dig up because no one really likes to admit she's jealous of what someone else has. Evidently, Rachel spent a lot of time counting Leah's baby blessings.

Since it takes nine months to have one baby, and Leah had four by the time Rachel sent her servant to Jacob to become pregnant, we can assume that Rachel spent at least four to five years watching Leah have baby after baby after baby.

Sometimes we understand very clearly what it's like to watch someone live out what we want the most, over and over and over.

When social media first started up, I would connect with everyone who connected with me. It seemed like the right thing to do at the time. But before I knew it, I had all these people in my life, and I wasn't sure I wanted them to be.

Thankfully my heart has grown enough to know I don't have to follow everyone all the time. We have to be protective about who we're letting into our lives. Even on social media.

How does social media affect your soul most days?

Do you feel like you have the freedom to unfollow accounts that stir up comparison in your heart? Why or why not?

Thankfully we live in a day and age where we can graciously exit people's social media lives if we want to. I'm not super crazy about people posting things like: "I just cut a lot of my friends. If you're seeing this you made the cut." But we can protect our hearts on social media and even in real life most days.

However, Rachel couldn't just unfollow Leah on social media. There was no way for her to not see what Leah was experiencing. This was her sister. And her sister-wife. They were in this thing together whether they wanted to be or not.

What is an example of a situation in which you are struggling with comparison that you cannot graciously exit?

Sometimes like Rachel and Leah, we find ourselves in an unfair comparison situation we cannot change. But that doesn't mean God just wants us to sit there and suffer silently through it. He's not an "Oh well" kind of God. He cares about every detail of our lives, including the details that stir up things in us that are not good.

Head to the Internet and look up the definition of these two words.

Envy:

Jealousy:

According to what you found, what are the differences between the two?

We don't have to let envy ruin us. We don't have to let jealousy control us. And we don't have to let unfair comparison situations in life lead us to do and say things that don't represent God well.

This isn't about winning. It's about walking through life well.

Our hope through this study is not that we'll completely get rid of comparison (because that's not happening), but that we will have the strength to combat it when it comes. In case you're struggling with an unfair situation today, here's a little plan to help you roll your sleeves up right now and get started in the fight.

1. When you think about your unfair situation, what is at least one thing you can be grateful for in the midst of it? Bonus points if you can think of three.

2. What does Romans 8:28 promise you about your unfair struggle?

3. Circle all the ways your unfair comparison struggle is harming you.
   Wasting time
   Creating a wedge in relationships
   Wasting energy
   Filling your thought life
   Making you focus on the bad instead of the good

4. What do you want to say to God about your unfair situation? Journal your answer.

TRUTH FOUR:

You didn't do anything wrong.

This week's Truth is powerful. When we see things through the lens of honesty (Truth One), see our situations like they really are (Truth Two), and accept that we don't always have to be OK (Truth Three), we are better able to grasp this week's truth. With Rachel and Leah, we have seen many of their circumstances were completely out of their control. They were trying to control the uncontrollable. But it only made things messy.

So as we pause for this mid-week truth check in, I want you to answer a few questions.

In what area(s) of your life are you so desperately trying not to compare and simply obey God, but things just don't seem to be working in your favor?

How is the outcome not looking like you had hoped?

Do you think you're ready to surrender the outcome or are you still in process? It's OK if you're still in this process, be honest about where you are.

Write out our Combating Comparison Verse for this week:

How is this verse going to help you in the future as you look at the situations in your life in which you've worked so hard toward one outcome, only to experience the opposite?

The Overthinkers

When Leah saw that she had stopped having children, she
took her slave Zilpah and gave her to Jacob as a wife.
GENESIS 30:9

Beginning Prayer:

_____

_____

_____

Confession: Hi, I'm Nicki—and I'm an overthinker.

It's true, you guys, I can overthink with the best of them. Normally my thoughts run to the worst place possible.

If my husband is running 15 minutes late and I can't get him on his phone? I start planning his funeral. My kids don't respond to my text message within approximately 35 seconds? I start pulling them up on our tracker app because I'm sure they have been kidnapped. I wasn't invited to that get-together happening live on my Instagram feed? They must not like me. Can you relate?

Overthinking happens to the best of us. But when we're in a comparison battle, it can wreck us. We try to make sense of everything. We want answers to our *why nots*? Sometimes we'll do whatever we have to do to get an answer.

After studying Rachel's and Leah's obsession with Jacob and with these babies, I couldn't help but wonder if they both belong to the overthinker club too. Today, we see this baby battle pick back up with Leah. But wait, didn't Leah surrender this thing? Didn't she decide she was going to praise God instead of pursuing this painful comparison process?

Where did we see Leah surrender?

Why do you think Leah is having a difficult time again?

READ GENESIS 30:9-12.

Who did Leah send to Jacob as a wife?

What was Leah's hope in giving her as his wife? (Check the clue in v. 9.)

What was the result? Circle the right answer.
    A. Three baby boys
    B. Two baby boys and one baby girl
    C. Two baby boys
    D. One baby boy

Verse 13 of this chapter gives us a clue into Leah's heart again. There's something stirring up in her that isn't good. Once again we see her words reflecting what's in her heart.

> Above all else, guard your heart, for everything you do flows from it.
> PROVERBS 4:23, NIV

Choosing to name the second baby Asher isn't the issue. It's the words that Leah shares with the announcement of his name that holds the struggle.

What reason does Leah give for his name (v. 13)?

Later we'll see that all the babies are all incredibly special and have a unique purpose in the roots of our faith. But I think we need to pause and see something important.

God's blessings for one person are never meant to be a burden for someone else.

Over and over these sisters are turning their babies into emotional burdens for one another. Leah isn't just happy because she's having another baby boy in her family. She's happy because she feels like she's proving a point, not only to her sister, but also to the women in her community.

This is one of the greatest dangers of comparison: turning God's blessings into a burden for someone else.

We've all experienced this. Someone's happiness making us unhappy. Or our happiness making someone else unhappy. We don't plan for it. We don't expect it. We don't even want to admit it most days. And for us overthinkers, we've especially got to be on guard. If we're not careful, we'll miss what God has right in front of us. The blessings. The dreams. The desires. He's got them just for us.

When has someone's blessing become a burden for you?

When has one of your blessings become a burden for someone else?

How can we be genuinely happy for others and ourselves without the source of that happiness turning into a burden?

I think we could list out some obvious things, such as don't brag or be insensitive to people around you. But there's something deeper I want us to experience today.

I really believe God wants to meet us in the quiet, secret places more than the public. I am a huge fan of sharing dreams and hopes with other people. It creates accountability and also provides encouragement when you need to keep going. But there are some things that are meant to just stay between God and me.

I know, this is not the message our tell-all world screams at us every day. If you open Facebook or Instagram right now (*don't!*) it will taunt you to tell someone something.

We take pictures of everything and everyone because most of us love to share our lives with someone. And there's nothing wrong with that.

But what if God just wants to take you on a journey that is just between you and Him?

Those deepest longings you have? I have them too. Those aches? Yep. Me too. Those prayers you're not sure God is hearing? Mmm hmm. And this desire to live out a life that is beyond myself? Everyday struggle.

My overthinking brain would love for me to just process those things all day. But the past few weeks I've really been letting God dig down deep into me. His work is not going to lead to a look-at-what-God-did-in-Nicki situation. In fact, you would be shocked to see what God is revealing in and through me.

It's painful. It's not pretty.

The more you stop staring at the success of others and focus in on what God is stirring in you, contentment will come. Will you be OK if this process never leads to anything more than just a deeper love and an understanding of God's love for you?

That's the difficult question. One every girl must wrestle with.

We'll keep wrestling tomorrow. See you then.

Manipulation Mandrakes

Reuben went out during the wheat harvest and found some
mandrakes in the field. When he brought them to his mother Leah,
Rachel asked, "Please give me some of your son's mandrakes."
GENESIS 30:14

Beginning Prayer:

_____

_____

_____

What's the craziest thing you've ever done for love?

I don't know if what I'm about to share falls into the category of crazy, but it definitely falls into the category of silly. When my husband and I were dating, we didn't get to spend a lot of time together. He worked full-time during the day as an electrician, and I had a part-time job at a nursing home in the evenings. One evening, my desperation to see him won out. I'm pretty sure I could have just called him and said I wanted to see him. But I felt like I needed a reason.

I completely made up some story about how we had a few extra cheeseburgers from the place with the golden arches, and I called him up to see if he wanted them. He said he absolutely did. Problem was, I didn't have any cheeseburgers. So, I quickly drove through the golden arches drive-thru and ordered three greasy cheeseburgers. But I was only a few minutes away, and if I arrived at his apartment with warm hamburgers, he'd be onto me.

Do you know what I did? Oh my word, it's so crazy to even write this out. I actually put them under my air conditioning vent in the car to cool them off!

Love has a way of making us do some of the craziest things. Some are funny, some are not.

Today's lesson, not super funny.

READ GENESIS 30:14-21.

What was the name of the son who had been working out in the field?

> A. Judah
>
> B. Reuben
>
> C. Levi
>
> D. Joseph

What did he find?

Have you ever heard of mandrakes before? Yes or No

I had not heard of them prior to studying this story, so I did a little digging around. Here are a few things I discovered.

FAST FACTS ABOUT MANDRAKES:
* It's a root-fruit.[1]
* It is also called "love apples" and Arabs often refer to them as "Satan's apples."[2]
* It was believed to help with infertility.[3]
* It was used as an anesthetic for surgery.[4]
* Most likely the root was boiled in wine to be consumed.[5]

What was Leah willing to do for one more opportunity to gain the love of Jacob?

Who actually ended up getting pregnant?

What does verse 20 say Leah's hope was after giving birth?

Poor Jacob. He seems to be the husband-for-hire. Going along with whatever these two combative sisters tell him. Leah ends up having two more sons, and then the first girl makes her way into this family.

What is the daughter's name (v. 21)?

READ GENESIS 30:22.

If we consider that Leah had three children between the mandrake incident and Rachel giving birth, we're looking at quite a bit of time between these two events. Rachel's manipulative mandrake situation didn't seem to work out too well for her.

And Leah's attempts to win Jacob's heart don't seem to be working either.

Let's go back one more time to our fourth Truth this week: *You didn't do anything wrong.* I'm seeing so clearly how much both of these women needed to hear this very specific truth at this very specific time.

If you could have had a conversation with Rachel and Leah, what would you have pointed out to show them they didn't do anything wrong to be experiencing the disappointment they were each experiencing?

Rachel	*Leah*

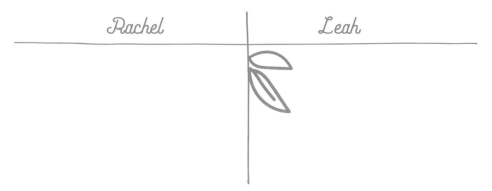

Neither one of these situations would be called doing something crazy for love. It's so much deeper than that for both of them. We could take sides and say one sister's situation was more difficult than the other's. But the reality is that over and over they were wanting what the other one had.

And they got to the point that they were willing to do whatever it took to win.

I don't know you, but I'm going to take my chances and say that I know a few things about you.

One, if you're doing this study, you are likely seeking God on some level. Two, you have probably encountered a lot of comparison as you've been doing this study. It seems like whenever we focus on a topic, it suddenly becomes a struggle that meets us every day. Here's the third thing I think I know about you: I don't think you're a manipulator. But I know you've been taunted by the one who manipulates, Satan.

So as we wrap up this week's study, I want to leave you with five ways manipulation can start to mess with us in the midst of comparison. I share this with you to help guard your heart against the manipulative efforts of the enemy. For ourselves and for what we could do to others.

> Below each action, give an example of something we've studied in Rachel and Leah's story so far that reveals them taking such action.
>
> 1. Feeling the need to stretch the truth. (AKA: Lie)
> Example:
>
> 2. Making things appear differently than they are.
> Example:
>
> 3. Pleading, begging, or demanding things be a certain way.
> Example:
>
> 4. Giving empty promises.
> Example:
>
> 5. Guilt tripping.
> Example:

You Be You

What is your Bible-phrase hashtag?

1. Your friends describe you as:
    A. Gutsy
    B. Contemplative
    C. Strong
    D. Cheery

2. You most often pray something similar to:
    A. "Lord, please help me overcome."
    B. "God, You are good even if this wasn't the path I wanted."
    C. "Help my unbelief because I trust You."
    D. "I want to hear You and know You."

3. You feel challenged by:
    A. How fast life goes because you enjoy the quiet, unrushed time with Him
    B. The big step God seems to be asking you to take
    C. Continuing to fight the good fight
    D. The temptation to keep a good attitude despite your circumstances

4. The Bible story that most resonates with you is:
    A. The Roman Centurion who amazed Jesus
    B. Paul and Silas singing in prison
    C. Jesus calming the stormy sea
    D. David and Goliath

5. Of the following songs, you are most likely to listen to:
    A. "Old Church Choir" by Zach Williams
    B. "Whom Shall I Fear [God of Angel Armies]" by Chris Tomlin
    C. "Thy Will" by Hillary Scott
    D. "Oceans [Where Feet May Fail]" by Hillsong United

RESULTS:

Question 1	Question 2	Question 3	Question 4	Question 5
A) 1	A) 3	A) 2	A) 1	A) 4
B) 2	B) 4	B) 1	B) 4	B) 3
C) 3	C) 1	C) 3	C) 2	C) 2
D) 4	D) 2	D) 4	D) 3	D) 1

Mostly 1s
#FaithCanMoveMountains

You are a maverick. You are going to go where God calls you to go and blaze a new trail. Keep your fierce faith and enjoy the adventure.

Mostly 2s
#BeStillAndKnow

You know that God sometimes speaks with a still, small voice, and you don't want to miss it! You value the holy pauses and quiet moments in His presence.

Mostly 3s
#MoreThanAConqueror

Life is challenging, but you are a steadfast fighter. Keep showing up for battle and putting on the armor of God. You know how the story ends! God has got this!

Mostly 4s
#ConsiderItPureJoy

Life has given you some heartache, but you are choosing to trust God. Keep choosing joy. Your attitude amidst the trial is making you shine all the brighter.

Week
five

TRUTH FIVE:

Her gain is not your loss.

COMBATING COMPARISON VERSE FIVE:

Rejoice with those who rejoice;
weep with those who weep.
ROMANS 12:15

Warm Things Up

Here are a few questions to get your group talking!

What are some things you learned from this week's personal study?

How did comparison show up in your life this week?

How active are you on social media? How is it a delight? How is it a downer? Do you have a good handle on it right now? Explain.

Are you an overthinker? How does that get you into trouble?

How have you applied the Combating Comparison Verse this week?

Watch

To hear more from Nicki, download the optional video bundle to view the Week Five teaching at www.LifeWay.com/RachelandLeah.

Create Conversation

Have you ever found yourself considering another woman's victory as a loss for you? If so, share a specific example with your group.

How does someone's blessing become a burden? Explain.

What are some realized and potential spiritual blind spots in your life? How can these do damage to your walk with Christ?

Is there a particular relationship or area of struggle that you feel tied down by? Explain. How can you can walk in freedom in this area?

What does the phrase "When she wins, we win. When she loses, we lose" mean to you? Does this perspective come easily? Why or why not?

End your time together allowing girls to share some personal wins and losses. For those who share wins, cheer them on. For those who share losses, circle around them and pray for them.

Facing Insecurity

After Rachel gave birth to Joseph, Jacob said to Laban,
"Send me on my way so that I can return to my homeland.
Give me my wives and my children that I have worked for,
and let me go. You know how hard I have worked for you."
GENESIS 30:25-26

Beginning Prayer:
Before you begin each study,
jot down a personal prayer here.

_____

_____

_____

I cringed when I heard the name of the woman leaving a voicemail. A woman of influence in our community was calling about something not-so-kind one of my daughters had done. She was quick to point out all the mistakes I had made in this situation and wasn't exactly the kindest soul.

I immediately began to feel insecure. So I did what every insecure woman does. I checked her Instagram to see how else I didn't measure up to this woman. And oh my, I found a dozen reasons. Her house, gorgeous. Her husband, madly in love with her. Her children, so lovely.

She definitely seemed to be winning at life.

Then as I clicked off her account and looked down at my feet, I saw that I desperately needed a pedicure. I looked around my house and saw just how much more needed to be fixed on the fixer-upper farm. I thought about this ordeal with my daughter and what this woman must think of me now—I just wanted to crawl back in bed and pull the covers over my eyes.

She was winning. And I was totally losing.

I know. These might seem like such childish thoughts. Someone might be thinking, *Come on Nicki, really?* But yeah, really.

I'm a grown woman, and there's nothing easy about admitting that I still look at other women and feel like I'm falling behind. Way behind.

Sure, I struggle with jealousy from time to time. But for me this struggle goes much deeper than jealousy. I really think it has to do with self-doubt.

If I'm honest, I really wonder sometimes if this world really needs another Bible teacher, another speaker, another book to read. It seems like it's all been covered by someone else— way better than I could ever cover it.

It's one thing to be a cheerleader for others, but it's another thing to stand on the sidelines of life. Wondering. Waiting. Hoping. Trying. Failing.

Do I really believe that if someone succeeds, it doesn't mean I lose?

It's an honest question—one I've had to wrestle with in the writing of this study. I can tell you, of all the truths we'll unpack in this study, this week's Truth changed me the most. And our Combating Comparison Verse this week has been a game changer in my life.

> Turn back to the first page of this week, and write out Truth Five and the Combating Comparison Verse.

I've stopped looking at someone's gain as my loss. I've come to understand what it means to rejoice with others and weep with others. Her gain is my gain. Her loss is my loss. And even when it's not returned, I've found the ability to not let the hurt I've felt from others' lack of enthusiasm over my life stop me from still cheering for them.

Don't misunderstand me. I am not suggesting you be fake and pretend to be happy when others succeed. I am suggesting you look to Jesus to change your heart.

READ GENESIS 30:25-36.

> Write down the key facts from this passage:

How had Jacob served Laban well?

Fill in the chart with the names of the babies we've read about so far.

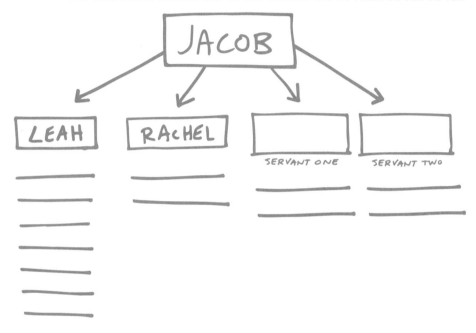

Why didn't Laban want them to leave?

A. Because he loved his grandkids so much

B. Because he knew he benefited from Jacob's work

C. Because he didn't want to lose Rachel and Leah

Too bad Laban had been such a sneaky, manipulative guy all the years Jacob had been with him. If he hadn't, then maybe Jacob would reconsider this deal. But good grief, Laban had done all he could do to get as much out of Jacob as he could.

It's like Laban thinks, *if Jacob goes, it all goes.* For just a second we're going to pause from our striving sisters and learn something from these two guys. Laban is insecure. Same type of insecurity I experienced the day I heard that voicemail. While my insecurity made me want to crawl in the bed and hide, Laban's made him into a bully.

I think if we took the time to trace back every form of manipulation we've initiated, we'd see some type of insecurity rooted deep inside us. There are a dozen roots of insecurity deep in my heart. Remember in Week One when I shared about my nineteen and pregnant story? That has been a deep place of rooted insecurity in me. I always feel like people look at my husband and me and think, *Oh they're a sweet couple. But you know, they had to get married.* Or, *Bless her heart, she was such a young mom. She just doesn't know any better.*

Granted, no one has ever said those words to me, but I'm telling you, insecurity has written some stories in my head.

But there came a day when I had to simply face my insecurity. I had to tell it to move on. I knew the assignment God had stirred inside me had to become stronger than the shouts of Satan in my head.

I faced my insecurity by finding and learning to love me. I mean it. Loving yourself in a way that honors God is one of the greatest steps we can take to overcome the manipulative tendencies insecurity stirs up in us.

It's why I've given you these fun little assessments on Day Five of each week. They're totally optional, but I really believe the more you know about yourself, the more you're gonna love who God made you to be. It's not self-centered to love who you are. To love God's design. It's actually biblical.

> Look up Psalm 139:14. What does it say we should do because God did such a good job creating us?

> Some of you will hate what I'm about to ask you to do, others will love it. Ready? OK, go ahead and list at least three things that you can praise God for about yourself. It may have to do with appearance, ideas you've had, ways you've loved other people well, or a million other things. But you can't skip this part. Don't. I'll find out—somehow. (*Wink*)
>
> 1.
>
> 2.
>
> 3.

Self-love and self-worship are two very different things. Proverbs 18:12 cautions us against letting pride convince us of our worth.

Before his downfall a person's heart is proud,
but humility comes before honor.
PROVERBS 18:12

What is the difference between self-love and self-worship?

Tomorrow we're going to see a big change for everyone in this story. See you there!

Desperate Desires

Then the LORD said to him, "Go back to the land of your
fathers and to your family, and I will be with you."
GENESIS 31:3

Beginning Prayer:

_____

_____

_____

I just didn't know how to respond to the text message my friend Michelle sent me.

Michelle is in her forties. She loves the Lord. She serves Him faithfully through various outlets in her life. She's blessed financially, and she is one of the smartest women I know. But there's an ache inside her.

Michelle has never been married. She has no children. And she's tired. Tired of not having a plus one to write on those wedding RSVPs. Tired of going to baby showers. Tired of watching other people have the life she wants while they seem so ungrateful for it all.

The night Michelle and I were texting back and forth about her aches, I so wished I had something to offer her. But words seemed to escape me.

Our Fifth Truth, the one we're working through this week is: *Her gain is not your loss.* But what do we do when someone's gain still feels like our loss?

Michelle said she could look at her life and see the things she could be grateful for. But bitterness was knocking at her door that night. She didn't want to answer, but it seemed like there was no other choice.

I was thinking so much about Rachel and Leah as Michelle and I were texting. Each sister repeatedly had to watch the other gain what she seemed to want the most. This is the part of the study where I'd love to become Coach Nicki. I'd love to blow my whistle and say,

"Alright girls! If you don't have what you want most in your life, it's time to get out there and get it!"

Wow. That sounds really good, but it's difficult to live out when time is passing so quickly and the life we always hoped to live isn't anywhere in sight.

Yes, I totally believe we should be consistently wrestling with God over our desires. He is a good God who wants to give us good things (Matt. 7:11). But the problem is we toss verses like Psalm 37:4 out there without a whole lot of thought about the substance and motivation of our desires.

> Take delight in the LORD, and he will give you your heart's desires.
> PSALM 37:4

Let's take a closer look at this verse because I think there's a really valuable truth for us here that we need to consider carefully.

READ PSALM 37:3-5.

In verse 3, the psalmist states that we are to "cultivate faithfulness" (NASB). What does that mean?

How do you "take delight in the Lord" (v. 4)?

In verse 5, what "way" is God asking you to commit to Him?

These verses weren't written while this story of Jacob, Laban, Leah and Rachel was unfolding, but I think there's a connection. At least with Jacob and Laban.

READ GENESIS 30:37–31:3.

After fourteen years of service to Laban, Jacob is ready to leave. He has done his time.

During this time, normally a master would send a servant away with extra material goods in hand. This keeps the servant from leaving empty-handed, so he doesn't have such a difficult time starting over. Laban should have provided for Jacob and his daughters and grandchildren by giving them something substantial as a send-off. But he doesn't want to.

Laban does not want to lose a good thing. He admits that he has benefited from Jacob's hard work. He wants to continue to reap blessings through Jacob.

So once again, Laban wants to work out a deal to keep Jacob. We studied this yesterday. But to recap: Jacob proposed to keep the speckled, spotted, and streaked animals from the flock as his payment. In a typical flock, normally the sheep would be white and the goats would be black or brown. Jacob wanted an easy way to distinguish the herds. Laban agreed.

Laban tried to reduce the chances of Jacob getting any of the spotted or speckled animals by removing them from the breeding stock that Jacob had to work with (Gen. 30:35-36). Jacob, however, had another plan.

What was Jacob's plan? List the facts from verses 37-40.

Do you think Jacob is manipulative or smart? Explain.

What ends up happening in verses 41-43?

What was Laban's reaction (Gen. 31:1-2)?

Fill in the blanks for verse 31:3:
The _____ said to him, "_____ back to the _____ of your _____ and to your _____, and ___ will _____ with _____."

We could definitely say Jacob tried to manipulate the outcome of the flocks' breeding by putting a visual stimulus in front of them when they came to the water troughs, the place the animals would usually mate.

Many commentators believe that Jacob is attempting to use "sympathetic magic," which would have nothing to do with a natural breeding practice.[2] We will see later, however, Jacob admits that these attempts had nothing to do with the outcome (Gen. 31:10-12).

There's a pattern here. Remember Rachel's manipulation mandrakes? Later we will see her pregnancy with Joseph had nothing to do with mandrakes.

Like Jacob and Rachel, until we recognize the sovereignty of God, we too will be tempted to try any means possible to fulfill the desires of our hearts. That includes things that followers of Jesus have no business doing (such as using good luck charms, etc.).

> What's the craziest old wives tale you've ever heard someone use to manipulate an outcome?

Sometimes these things are silly. Like the January when someone on Facebook said if we wanted it to snow in Charlotte, NC, (*because it almost never does!*) we should all sleep with spoons under our pillows! Unfortunately, sometimes we easily dismiss logic and, more tragically, God's truth to try to find a way to fulfill our desires.

Part of our problem is trying to put God into formulas. Our logical brains need answers to life's nos. We need responses to give to friends like Michelle who are honestly struggling to find peace when everyone else seems to be winning.

I love the last part of today's study passage. Because God tells Jacob, *It's time to go home.* God saw it all. All the lies. All the manipulation. All the hard work. All the fear. Every bit of Jacob's journey. God saw it. And then, enough was enough.

I wonder if God's calling us to return to this sacred place in our lives today.

I hope you're seeing what I'm seeing in this story. No one is living it out perfectly. In fact, there's a lot more imperfection than perfection. But God's love is still being intertwined through it. And not just His love, but His blessing.

And while I don't have an answer to give Michelle, I know I can pray for God's blessing over her life. I don't know what blessing God sees as best for her, but I know I want it for her. And I want it for you too.

MID-WEEK TRUTH CHECK-IN

TRUTH FIVE:
Her gain is not your loss.

This week we are discovering how to not see others' gains as our loss. This truth is widely needed in this competitive culture we find ourselves in. I really believe one of the greatest ways we live out this truth in our lives is by really understanding our Combating Comparison Verse this week.

Fill in the blanks for Romans 12:15

_____ with those who _____ ;

_____ with those who _____ .

> **FAST FACT:**
> Cross-referencing means referencing another text or part of a text, typically given in order to elaborate on a point.

Whenever we're studying a verse in the Bible, it's always great to do some cross-reference studying to help us gain a better picture of what this verse is explaining to us.

Turn to Ecclesiastes 3:4. What are the four things this verse tells us there's a time for?

1. _____

Give an example of a time you did this with someone:

2. _____

Give an example of a time you did this with someone:

3. _____

Give an example of a time you did this with someone:

4. _____

Give an example of a time you did this with someone:

Circle the words you think best fit in the category of not seeing someone's gain as your loss.

Compassion   Sympathy   Hope

Trust   Gladness   Celebrate

Forgiveness   Integrity   Rejoice

Which of those words do you find yourself struggling with the most? Why?

Look back at our Combating Comparison Verse and Ecclesiastes 3:4. What are some specific ways God is asking you to work through Romans 12:15 at this point in your life?

Leaving Laban

Then Rachel and Leah answered him,
"Do we have any portion or inheritance in our father's family?"
GENESIS 31:14

Beginning Prayer:

_____

_____

_____

OK, so we're not in a boxing match, but this week's study kind of feels like it. If I could, I would ding the bell and shout, "In this corner, we have Jacob. And in corner number two, we have Laban." We have seen these men go round and round. Today's study isn't ending that battle just yet.

READ GENESIS 31:4-21.

What reasons did Jacob give for why they needed to leave?

What are the questions both Rachel and Leah asked in verses 14-16?

Rachel and Leah felt like they had been treated as outsiders and had no attachment to their father's family. Technically, Laban should have saved some or most of the bride price Jacob worked so hard for, but he didn't. He had spent it.[3]

Here's something so interesting. The word for *outsiders* in verse 15 literally means *foreigners*.[4] This is the same word Ruth would later use to describe herself when talking about the unexpected way Boaz had treated her, an outsider, with such consideration and kindness (Ruth 2:10-11).[5]

Except, this crew is experiencing the complete opposite of Boaz's kindness. It's definitely not right, for Jacob to be treated as an outsider after 20 years of loyal service, but it really is inexcusable for Laban's daughters to be treated this way.

If Romans 12:15 had been written at this point in Jacob and Laban's battle, I'm not sure they would have applied it. There were things that happened on both sides that weren't right or fair, and definitely didn't reflect the heart of God.

See, that's the thing about this comparison battle. We often don't realize it's a battle for us until it's too late. My hope for you is that this study is bringing your struggle to light, so you can have a plan when comparison shows up uninvited at your school, at practice, or the next time you scroll through social media.

But before we close out today, there's one more not-right thing we need to see happen.

What does Genesis 31:19 say Rachel stole?

Why do you think it's Rachel, and not Leah, that did this?

According to the customs of that time, Rachel had the right to an inheritance. But that doesn't mean she had the right to do what she did. It could be that her sense of entitlement led her to steal what she thought might give her protection on the journey or possibly even another pregnancy. Her action could have cost her life.

Are you on the edge of your seat? Me too!

See you tomorrow as we read one of the most shocking parts of this whole story.

Comparison's High Cost

Now you have gone off because you long for your father's family—
but why have you stolen my gods?

GENESIS 31:30

Beginning Prayer:

_____

_____

_____

Not too long after we bought the fixer-upper farm, I decided I was going to have a little Christmas party. I'll be honest, I was in major comparison mode. It was the first time so many of my friends were going to see our house. No one intentionally made me feel this way, but I had written a story in my head about their high expectations of our house and felt like I needed to do everything I could to meet them.

I cleaned and decorated for days. I searched high and low on Pinterest® for all the perfect food ideas. I bought new pillows for the couch, art for the walls, and fresh hand towels for the bathroom. I made my people put their shoes away.

The day of the party arrived and I awoke with such excitement. But that excitement was quickly extinguished as I took a deep breath. There was an aroma filling the air that smelled nothing like sugar and spice and everything nice. I nudged my husband to get up, and we began the great smell hunt. We followed our noses all the way upstairs where my nostrils confirmed there was something dead. In. Our. House.

I panicked, thinking: *What could be dead upstairs?*

Kris, my husband, climbed through the attic searching, but he couldn't find anything. Then we realized what had happened. Apparently a mouse had made its way upstairs and taken it's last breath somewhere inside the corner wall. There was no getting that mouse out unless we cut the drywall open.

Not an option with a party only a few hours away. So, on a thirty-degree day, I did what every sane woman throwing a Christmas party with a dead mouse in her wall would do. I opened every window, put oils in every diffuser I owned, and lit every candle I had. I plugged in every air freshener I could find and sprayed every room with as much fragrance spray as I could.

I needed this day to be perfect. And this stupid mouse was messing it all up. Why did I need things to be so perfect?

Because I wanted to impress *her*. She was coming. *Her*, this woman I constantly find myself in comparison's shadow with. She's beautiful, smart, funny, wealthy, and wise. I was sure *she'd* never had a dead mouse make her entire house stink.

Because mice favor people, you know?

The party was fine. The smell was masked well. But when I laid my head down to sleep that night, I was exhausted. And for what? To impress *her?*

That's the thing with comparison—it demands us to do more, be better, look our best, and strive full speed ahead. But, for what? Comparison ends up costing us a whole lot more than we'd ever imagine.

Your party is perfectly planned and decorated, but what did it cost you? Wishing you'd never invite someone over again?

The outfit looks amazing, but what did it cost you? Time? Money? Your thoughts? Was the cost worth it?

You finally got that guy you like to notice you. But what did it almost cost you? Time? Your though life? Your friendships with others? Was it worth it?

Comparison brings a cost we rarely count or consider. Until it's too late.

When has comparison cost you something?

Rachel got the idols she wanted, but what did it almost cost her? Let's find out.

READ GENESIS 31:22-35.

What did God say to Laban in his dream (v. 24)?

How is this a fulfillment of what God said to Jacob in Genesis 28:12-15?

Do you believe Laban would have really let Jacob, Rachel, and Leah leave peacefully? Why or why not?

I love that God told Laban he'd better not mess with Jacob (v. 29)! I think this is one of my favorite parts of this story. Laban was a bit dramatic in accusing Jacob of taking his daughters off like prisoners of war. He's all like, "I need to kiss my grandkids goodbye!" What? I'm sure there was some eye rolling when those words rolled out of Laban's mouth.

Then, in almost an "Oh by the way" type of response, Laban says:

> Now you have gone off because you long for your father's family—
> but why have you stolen my gods?
> GENESIS 31:30

Jacob states that he didn't take Laban's idols, and if Laban can find anyone with Jacob who did, Jacob would kill them. Well now. This is an interesting situation, isn't it?

Whose tent did Laban go into to search for the idols first, second, third, and fourth (Gen. 31:33)?

1.

2.

3.

What happened when Laban went into Rachel's tent (Gen. 31:35)?

Did you laugh when you read that? I totally did. I mean, all a girl had to do is say it was her special time of the month, and the man is G-O-N-E.

The truth is, God intervened to save Rachel, but not because he thought her theft of idols was OK. He intervened because He had plans for Jacob and his family.

What do you think Rachel's reaction was after Laban walked out of the tent?

A. Relieved

B. Scared

C. Disappointed in herself

Do you think if Jacob had known it was Rachel he would have said the same thing? Explain.

Later, in Genesis 35:2, we see that Jacob orders all his family and servants to get rid of their idols. He buries them under a tree. Enough is enough.

Sometimes comparison convinces us to do whatever we have to do and say whatever we need to say to get ahead. Rachel's comparison mode almost cost her life.

I'm super excited about where we're heading next week in this study. No, Rachel's and Leah's story isn't going to be tied up with a pretty bow and placed in your lap. It ends messy. But we're going to see some type of restoration for everyone.

Before we end this week, I want you to really take some time to understand what can happen when you constantly see other people's gains as your loss. Embracing this truth, that her gain is not your loss, is one of the greatest places God can start to restore your soul from this comparison compromise.

When a girl struggles to understand the goodness of God in her life, she will always look at another girl's success as a threat. Those threats can make us do some crazy things.

Today, I want you to fill in this chart and discover all the good gains God has given you. Hopefully this will help you see what God is doing in your life and help you celebrate what God is doing in *her* life. This will help keep the compromise of comparison away.

WAYS I HAVE SEEN GOD'S GOODNESS IN MY LIFE THIS PAST WEEK	WAYS I HAVE SEEN GOD'S GOODNESS IN MY LIFE TODAY	WAYS I WILL CONTINUE TO LOOK FOR GOD'S GOODNESS IN MY LIFE

You Be You

What are you excited about?

1. You are in the church gym with a large group of kids for an event, you are most excited about:
    - A. Playing with the kids and asking them questions
    - B. Quietly rearranging the coats or shoes and staying away from the group
    - C. Gathering a group of kids to play an organized game
    - D. Turning up the music in order to enhance the event
    - E. Introducing yourself to the parents and kids you don't know
    - F. Wiping off counters and serving punch
    - G. Planning the night or next children's event with the other leaders
    - H. Finding a way to share the gospel with someone there

2. You are having coffee at a local coffee shop with five friends. Three of them are old friends; two of them are girls you've never met. One of them brought her little sister. You are most interested by:
    - A. Quietly listening to what everyone is talking about
    - B. Focusing on the new girls and asking them questions
    - C. Planning the next gathering
    - D. Bringing up deep biblical questions and inviting the new girls to church
    - E. Keeping the little sister company while the others talk
    - F. Driving the conversation and bringing up new topics
    - G. Seeing if any of them play an instrument or sing
    - H. Making sure everyone is enjoying their coffee

3. Your family is planning a camping vacation, you'll most likely:
   A. Make a list of all the possible destinations and take a hands-on approach
   B. Be the first in the car and you'll get a fire started as soon as you arrive
   C. Look forward to some quiet, alone time when you get there
   D. View the campground as your mission field
   E. Put in a vote for a campsite near a waterpark
   F. Say hello to your campsite neighbors when you arrive
   G. Download new music or bring a new book for the road trip
   H. Ask others where they want to go before giving your own opinion

4. On a normal Sunday at church, you are mostly likely:
   A. Sitting anywhere but the front
   B. Finding new faces and inviting them to hang out after
   C. On stage with the worship team or doing special music
   D. In the nursery
   E. Leading a Bible study
   F. Making sure everything is running smoothly
   G. Greeting people at the door or shaking hands with newcomers
   H. Emptying trash cans or stacking chairs

5. On a mission trip, you'd be most excited about:
   A. Getting to know a culture or city that you know nothing about
   B. Painting, building, or digging something for someone
   C. Sharing the gospel with people
   D. Deciding where the team will be going and developing an itinerary
   E. Helping wherever needed—just don't ask me to pray in front of the team
   F. Worshiping in a new environment
   G. Helping hurting kids and showing them love
   H. Making sure everyone gets the most out of this trip

Question 1	Question 2	Question 3	Question 4	Question 5
A) - 1	A) - 2	A) - 7	A) - 2	A) - 5
B) - 2	B) - 5	B) - 6	B) - 8	B) - 6
C) - 3	C) - 7	C) - 2	C) - 4	C) - 8
D) - 4	D) - 8	D) - 8	D) - 1	D) - 7
E) - 5	E) - 1	E) - 1	E) - 3	E) - 2
F) - 6	F) - 3	F) - 5	F) - 7	F) - 4
G) - 7	G) - 4	G) - 4	G) - 5	G) - 1
H) - 8	H) - 6	H) - 3	H) - 6	H) - 3

Mostly 1s

You're excited about being with kids.

Mainly 2s

You're excited about unseen work.

Mainly 3s

You're excited about leading.

Mainly 4s

You're excited about music/audio.

Mainly 5s

You're excited about new relationships.

Mainly 6s

You're excited about physical tasks.

Mainly 7s

You're excited about decision-making.

Mainly 8s

You're excited about outreach.

How can I use this excitement for God and His purpose?

In order to better take care of myself, is there anything I
am currently involved in that I'm not excited about? Is this a
commitment I need to see through or let go of now?

Based on these results, what activities or mission projects should I
sign up for in the future?

Week
Six

TRUTH SIX:

Let the success and struggles of others encourage, not discourage, you.

COMBATING COMPARISON VERSE SIX:

We do not dare to classify or compare ourselves with some who commend themselves. When they measure themselves by themselves and compare themselves with themselves, they are not wise.

2 CORINTHIANS 10:12 (NIV)

Warm Things Up

Here are a few questions to get your group talking!

What are some things you learned from this week's personal study?

How did comparison show up in your life this week?

What are some things you praise God for about yourself? Do you find it difficult to think of anything? Explain.

How have you seen God's goodness in your life this past week?

How have you applied the Combating Comparison Verse this week?

Watch

To hear more from Nicki, download the optional video bundle to view the Week Six teaching at www.LifeWay.com/RachelandLeah.

Create Conversation

Do you ever find yourself turning models into idols? How might you keep those models in their rightful place in your heart?

Why is it important to remember that most people's successes didn't happen overnight?

In moments of insecurity and comparison, what would it take for you to hear God's voice louder than the voice of comparison? What keeps you from believing God?

Is it disappointing or encouraging to you to know that Rachel's and Leah's story doesn't end happily ever after? Explain.

How might another girl's success be an encouragement to you?

Pray that the loudest voice in the ears and hearts of the girls in your group will be the voice of God. Pray they will have open, teachable hearts to hear Him.

Where God Speaks

God said to Jacob, "Get up! Go to Bethel and settle
there. Build an altar there to the God who appeared
to you when you fled from your bother Esau."
GENESIS 35:1

Beginning Prayer:
Before you begin each study,
jot down a personal prayer here.

Where do you feel God speaks to you the most?

It's an honest question that I'm not sure we really take the time to answer. I love getting away to spend time alone with God. Many of the words in this Bible study were written in my friend's cabin because I needed space to hear from God without distraction. Please understand, most of my life happens at home—with kids, dogs, donkeys, and pigs all around me.

I don't really have the luxury of going away anytime I need to hear from God.

So, I have specific things I do when I need to really lean into the presence of God. First, I worship. Then, perhaps because I'm a creative person, closing my eyes, lifting my hands, and picturing the throne room of heaven really helps me get to a place where I'm ready to listen.

Next, I open the Bible. I study a lot for the various roles I have in ministry. I used to feel guilty for using the passages I was teaching or writing on as personal study passages. But now, I don't want to teach on a passage unless I've personally wrestled with it. So I will read a passage or listen to a sermon on the text I'm studying.

Lastly, I pray. I write names, words, and ideas down in my journal. Sometimes I draw circles around the names as I pray so that I can pray specifically. Then sometimes I drop to my knees and get flat on my face in prayer.

It looks different each time I encounter God, but there are threads of similarity each time.

What does your routine or rhythm of meeting with God look like?

Sometimes when I'm reading the Bible and I see how God spoke to people like Jacob, I can get a little unsure about the way I think God speaks to me. I guess you could say it's a comparison I make.

I mean, I do have some donkeys He could speak through (Num. 22:21-39). And our farm has a few bushes that could start burning (Ex. 3). I've also promised God if an angel appeared to me I would *not* freak out (Luke 1:26-38).

I've accepted that, most likely, God isn't going to speak to me those ways. It would be great, but it's probably not happening today. Instead, I've had to find my space with God. I'm learning to listen and lean into God's presence in my office, car, a coffee shop, or wherever else I am.

We're going to see God speaking to Jacob in a powerful way today. But first, let's find out what happened with Jacob and Laban.

READ GENESIS 31:43-55.

List at least four key points from those verses.

1.

2.

3.

4.

What are your thoughts about the covenant they made?

How did Jacob and Laban's encounters with God affect
this outcome?

I think it's so interesting that the times we studied Rachel and Leah speaking of God, what they said wasn't always the best reflection of God's character. We saw them claiming that God would give or had given what they wanted most, love and babies. For example,

> Leah conceived, gave birth to a son, and named him
> Reuben, for she said, "The LORD has seen my affliction;
> surely my husband will love me now."
> GENESIS 29:32

> Rachel said, "God has vindicated me; yes, he has heard
> me and given me a son," so she named him Dan.
> GENESIS 30:6

In the passage for today, we see moments of humility where Jacob and Laban make peace with each other before God.

What does humility before God look like for you?

How has God been speaking to you throughout this study about
the situations where you tend to compare yourself with others?
How does humility play a role in what God is showing you?

I think it's great we're seeing peace finally come, great for everyone. I wish I could tell you there's a whole lot more to uncover about Rachel and Leah in this story, but the Bible gets pretty quiet about them for a few chapters.

We are introduced to many more characters and situations from Genesis 32–35. I encourage you to read through those chapters and let God keep speaking to you about this story. But for time's sake, we're going to speed up to the end of this story. I know, such a bummer. I love hanging out with you! But there's some good stuff ahead that I just can't wait to show you.

Tomorrow we're going to see something powerful happen with this family. Then we're going to see things get a little sad.

Because we've got a lot to unpack this week, I want to get our Combating Comparison Verse in front of you first thing. This verse was an anchor for me when I was wrestling with God over the writing of this study. God used this verse to speak to me about the comparison struggle in my life.

But rather than just study the verse this week, I want us to look at most of the chapter where our verse comes from.

READ 2 CORINTHIANS 10.

> We do not dare to classify or compare ourselves with some who commend themselves. When they measure themselves by themselves and compare themselves with themselves, they are not wise.
>
> 2 CORINTHIANS 10:12 (NIV)

Read this verse aloud.

Circle all the words in this verse that are action words.

Put a box around the advice given.

This verse was written by Paul, a very wise teacher of the gospel. Most of his teachings in the Bible come in the form of a letter. He was also widely criticized in his work of spreading the gospel. Some of his sharpest criticism came from the people in the church at Corinth, to whom Paul wrote the letters we know as First and Second Corinthians.

How does being criticized often lead to more comparison in our lives?

How can criticism hurt our ability to listen well to God?

The tenth chapter of 2 Corinthians opens with humility and gentleness, but Paul quickly moves into his discussion of spiritual warfare and defending his spiritual authority. Sometimes we do need to keep our eyes on those who are ahead of us. There are things we can learn from them. But we've got to be careful that our humility doesn't turn into pride.

Maybe you're already familiar with the phrase *humble brag*. If not, it's when someone says something meant to come across in a humble way, but it's really bragging. They say something good about themselves, but disguise it as if they are being humble. It's self-promotion in it's worst form.

Example: *I'm exhausted from my two-week vacation in Hawaii. I need a vacation from my vacation.*

Unless we really grasp what true humility looks like, this week's Truth, *Let the success of others encourage not discourage you*, is going to be difficult to understand. It's this fine line of learning to celebrate the success of others while staying in your own lane. It's also learning from others while not letting comparison compromise what God is doing in you.

Write out any thoughts or prayers you have after reading 2 Corinthians 10. What are some areas of your life in which God is showing you that you need to have a spirit of humility? What other verses on humility are there in the Bible? Use the space below to process this.

Go To That Place

Jacob named the place where God had spoken with him Bethel.
GENESIS 35:15

Beginning Prayer:

_____

_____

_____

I'm thirty-seven years old at the time of writing this study. I think the late thirties are a weird phase of life. You're a little wiser than you used to be, but there's still so much to learn.

The other night I was at a birthday party with my friend Meg. Meg is a woman who loves to cook, and she's a good one too! Me on the other hand? I'm lucky if I don't burn the frozen lasagna. I want to be a good cook, but I just don't seem to have a knack for it.

So I admire Meg. As she and I were chatting at the party, it turns out Meg admires my decorating style. I had no idea. She's building a new house and wanted my help on a few things.

I was over the moon excited to offer up my opinion. Meg made me an offer. She said, "Help me with my decorating, and I'll teach you a few things about cooking." Honestly, I'd like to just *hire* Meg to cook for me (*wouldn't that be nice?*), but I loved her offer to skill swap with me.

Everyone in life has something to teach us. And we've got something to teach someone else. But do we look at life that way? Or are we only looking at how we can get ahead?

I think Laban, Jacob, Leah, and Rachel all struggled with trying to get ahead. But we're finally seeing this thing turn around, at least for a little while.

READ GENESIS 35:1-8.

Where did God tell Jacob to go?

Why is this place significant?

What was he supposed to do there?

What are the three instructions Jacob gave his family (v. 2)?

1.

2.

3.

Then what would they do (v. 3)?

We have to be careful that we don't get into a legalistic mindset with God. When we study things like this it's easy to think, "*Oh OK. Well, they did A, B, and C. Then God showed up.*" I do believe there's something we can learn from this, which leads me to sharing our sixth and final truth for our study:

Let the success of others encourage, not discourage, you.

We've learned so much from Rachel and Leah's comparison struggle. There's still a pretty big lesson to learn, and we're getting there. But today feels like a win for this family. Laban and Jacob have settled their struggles. Jacob has heard from God and is leading his family well because of these encounters.

I'm seeing a hint of success coming forward.

The problem with success is that it's often defined in the eyes of the beholder. And so the question is, *Who are we letting define our success?*

This world? Ourselves? Or God?

We're going to see an incredible line of godly success come from this family. But for today, I think it's incredibly significant to see this moment of success.

READ GENESIS 35:9-15.

What is the new name God gave Jacob?

What was the promise God gave him in verse 11?

Jacob named this place where God spoke to him Bethel.

This is the place where the striving stopped. The comparisons were no longer compromising what God was trying to do through everyone. It was where humility was joined with honor to create an atmosphere where God could move.

Maybe today we need to find our Bethel.

Comparison. Wrong attitudes. Competition. Unconfessed sins. Resentment. These are the things that can keep us from learning from someone else. They will keep us in a pattern of falling behind when trying to measure up.

I want to help you find this place in your soul where you can rest and release this comparison thing.

I texted two questions to a few of my friends. I consider all these women and girls to be successful, and there's a lot I've learned from them. I want you to do the same. Here are the questions I asked: 1) What is the number one thing you compare yourself in? and 2) How has comparison made you miss what God was doing in you?

Here's a few of their responses:

"As the only single woman in a group of married friends, I often compared myself to the life they were living and the life I wanted to live. This led me to make bad choices because I was pursuing what I thought I needed instead of allowing God to work. There was good that came from that season but also a lot of personal regret over the decisions I made I've had to release." -GW

"I struggle with comparison in my grades. It's distracted me from what God is teaching me specifically and what I should actually be getting out of school! I've let it make me think my brain isn't as good or important as other people's because I don't make the same grades as them. But it's also taught me how to look for my own gifts in life, instead of other people's." -BH

"My biggest area of comparison is body image. Growing up in ballet, I spent thousands of hours in front of a mirror in a leotard and tights, during the most transformative time of my body as a young girl. That feeling of inadequacy and jealousy hasn't gone away as I've entered my 30s. But now I can see that if Satan can keep me preoccupied with hating my physical body, he can keep me distracted from my calling. My job is to equip women. And I believe that God has allowed thick thighs and a squishy tummy to make me relatable to other women. I understand how they feel because I've felt it too, and I look like them. The average American woman is a size 16! So they trust me, and I earn the right to be heard. It's a cool moment to realize that my shape is a part of the way God has equipped me to grow the kingdom!" -WM

"I want to do my best, but comparison keeps me from seeing my full value in the eyes of God. I doubt my self-worth and value if I'm not achieving the perfection I desire. But it has also allowed me to see how unconditionally I am loved despite my lack of ability and failures. I'm not meant to be perfect and never will be. Comparison makes it seem like others are perfect even when they're falling short just like you." -AC

I share these comments with you to help you see that comparison really can compromise our God assignments. No matter what those assignments look like. Hopefully there's something you can learn from these comments, some encouragement you can gain. A place you can rest your soul.

TRUTH SIX:

Let the success of others encourage, not discourage, you.

Comparison creates a posture in our hearts. Most of the time that posture becomes one of bowing down to the wrong things. Success can definitely be one of those things we start to bow down to.

But sometimes when we compare, it can show us that something is possible.

I've noticed something about women. Whenever we meet someone for the first time, we typically share what we do. In those moments, if a woman feels inferior to another woman she'll take the, "Oh wow, I could never do what you do," route.

It's true there are some things we are just not created to do! You will never find me singing on TV or even in front of a church. Have mercy, no. I am not created to be a signer.

I don't think that seed of comparison really shows up when we meet someone who's doing something we know we aren't made to do. It typically shows up when we meet someone else whose doing what we know we want to do.

But behind every successful woman is a story. A story she is most likely to share with you, if you'll ask her.

Write down the name of the most successful adult you know or someone you really admire (a real-life person, someone you could actually have a conversation with).

What are the qualities about this person that you compare yourself to?

Have you ever asked them what helped them become successful in that area you admire? Yes or No? If no, why not?

Whether you answered yes or no to that question, let me give you three great questions to ask the adult you admire. Her answers should help you let her success encourage and not discourage you. Go ahead, be brave. Text that person. Call her. Offer to buy her lunch. Do whatever you have to do to learn from her.

1. What was it like when you first started doing what you do?

2. Who inspired you?

3. What was the best/worst decision you ever made?

A New Name

> With her last breath—for she was dying—she named
> him Ben-oni, but his father called him Benjamin.
> **GENESIS 35:18**

Beginning Prayer:

_____

_____

_____

In Week Three of this study, I shared that I was going through one of the hardest seasons of my life with my mom. It's with tears streaming down my face today that I write these final words to this study. My mom is no longer with us. Her struggle is over. Her suffering has ended and she has met Jesus.

For that, I am grateful. But the last fifteen days of my mom's life were brutal. She had stopped eating and drinking. She was on morphine. She couldn't speak. She couldn't see. She was in a lot of pain. It was the worst two weeks of my life.

So today's lesson is a little raw on my soul. I now know a little too well what it's like to be by someone's side when life is ending.

It's been quite a journey for Rachel and Leah. What started off as two young girls in a battle for love is ending with more than a dozen kiddos running around, a lot of drama, and learning to live life outside of their father's influence.

We don't see them making peace with each other. We don't see Jacob finally giving Leah his love. And we don't see this comparison battle end. Even up until the last moment.

READ GENESIS 35:16-20.

Where were they traveling to when Rachel gave birth?

What did Rachel's midwife say to her when the birth became difficult?

Do a search on Google and look up the meaning of the name Ben-oni.

It means: Son of my _____.

Unlike the situation with my mom, where death was the expected outcome after a six-month battle, Rachel's death wasn't expected at all. But death is death. Loss is loss.

Here's what I know—at the end of someone's life, you're not tossing around all the things that person said to you that hurt your feelings. In fact, most of the time, those things are quickly forgotten. We tend to focus on the good parts of that person's life and what we're going to miss the most.

When someone dies, we're left with the aftermath. And grief can be the worst friend, following us around everywhere we go. Popping up out of nowhere. Showing up at the worst times.

I wonder how Rachel's death affected Leah. Did she wish she could have said something differently? When Rachel's baby cried, did she hold him? Were there added responsibilities to her now that Rachel was gone? What would life look like from that point on?

I think one of the greatest lessons we can learn from the struggle between these sisters is that comparison stole a lot from them. There was a lot of hurt inside both of them that was never healed.

Have you ever thought about what you want your life to look like in your final moments? Do you want it to be filled with sorrow or peace?

I know we would all say we want peace. But considering where you are now with yourself, others, and God, is that what you would experience? I don't think all comparison has to make us feel horrible and force us to live our lives in a way that leads us to sorrow.

Even though this is a very sad ending to this story, something beautiful happened in the middle of this mess.

> What does Genesis 35:18 say Jacob changed his baby's name to?

Jacob is sad. He is full of sorrow. But there is no way he's letting his child carry the burden of being named *Son of My Sorrow*. Jacob gave him a new name. Something God did for him (Gen. 35:10). Jacob gave his son a name of hope and strength: *Son of the Right Hand,* or *Benjamin.*

Sometimes we need to give our struggles a new name. I could have looked at that heart-breaking season with my mom as a punishment. Sometimes it felt that way. But I can honestly tell you, walking with my mom through those six months, and even those last fifteen days, was a privilege.

But I still struggle. Even today comparison tried to mess with me.

I got teary eyed when I called my friend and she said, "Oh, can I call you back, I'm having lunch with my mom right now." I let the tears fall, wishing I could have lunch with my mom. Then I remembered—it was a privilege, not a punishment, to have that time with her.

Thankfully God placed two really good friends ahead of me who experienced their own seasons of grief. One lost her dad about two months before I lost my mom. The other lost her mom two weeks before I lost mine. It's helped to follow in their steps and learn what grief has taught them so it can teach me as well.

> In the same way, I think we can learn from this grief-filled situation in the story of Rachel and Leah. What is the new name you need to give your struggle?

How can you redefine this season?

What can you learn from someone who has walked this road before you?

I really believe those three questions will help lead us to a place of peace rather than sorrow. Hold tight, there's still goodness coming.

Party of 12

Jacob had twelve sons: Leah's sons were Reuben (Jacob's firstborn), Simeon, Levi, Judah, Issachar, and Zebulun. Rachel's sons were Joseph and Benjamin. The sons of Rachel's slave Bilhah were Dan and Naphtali. The sons of Leah's slave Zilpah were Gad and Asher. These are the sons of Jacob, who were born to him in Paddan-aram.

GENESIS 35:23-26

Beginning Prayer:

_____

_____

_____

Well, it's not a happily ever after for Jacob, Rachel, or Leah. But that doesn't mean something good isn't going to come from all they've experienced. In fact, it's not just something good coming but something great!

In order for us to see the coming celebration, we're going to need to look back. This isn't something you're going to want to skip over, it's so good!

TURN TO GENESIS 22:1-18. READ THOSE VERSES AND ANSWER THESE QUESTIONS.

1. What is the name of Jacob and Essau's father?

2. He was _____ son (vv. 1-2).

3. Why was Abraham going to sacrifice him?

4. What was the promise God gave Abraham after God told him not to touch Issac (vv. 17-18)?

READ GENESIS 35:11 AND FILL IN THE BLANKS:

God also said to him, "I am _____ _____. Be
_____ and _____. A nation, indeed an _____
of _____, will come from _____, and
_____ will descend from you."

NOW TURN TO GENESIS 49:1-33. READ THOSE VERSES.

I know it's a lot of verses to read and on the last day of study! (*You are so rolling your eyes at me.*) But I don't want you to miss this! It's *so good.*

Jacob's party of twelve would grow up and become the foundation of our faith. They would build the twelve tribes that would eventually form the nation of Israel.

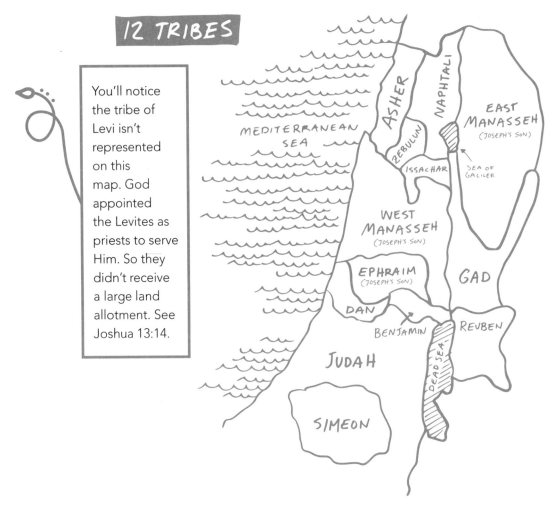

12 TRIBES

You'll notice the tribe of Levi isn't represented on this map. God appointed the Levites as priests to serve Him. So they didn't receive a large land allotment. See Joshua 13:14.

Israel. The place where Jesus would one day be born, live, and die on a cross for you and for me. And the place where Jesus will one day return.

God had a plan, and nothing was going to stop it. No lying, stealing, cheating, kicking, screaming, comparing, or even despising would stop His good plans for this family.

God still has a plan, and nothing will stop it. No evil. No deception. Nothing.

I love this so much. Honestly, there is so much more we could talk about with these twelve tribes and what God did through them.

TURN TO RUTH 4:11.

Who do the people and elders say they hope Ruth will be like?

There's a theme we see throughout the Bible. God often shows up in the messiest of places and makes the most beautiful things. Our hope is the same as the elders of Ruth—that the life we're building will point people to eternity.

There are some messes in your life and in my life from which we need God to make something good. So let God do what He needs to do through *her* life. Let God do what he needs to do in *your* life. Don't let comparison make you miss it. Like Rachel, Leah, and Ruth, we may never see on this earth what God will do through our generational lines. But if we'll stay faithful to the process, God will fulfill His purpose.

The thing is, He'll do it with or without us. Now I don't know about you, but I don't want to miss it.

So:
- For the girl who has believed the lie of comparison, that she's too young, age is nothing but a number (1 Tim. 4:12).

  - For the woman who believed the lie of comparison, that her best days are behind her, with God, the best is always yet to come (1 Cor. 2:9).

  - For the girl who has believed comparison's lie and can never seem to get with the program, He makes all things new (2 Cor. 5:17).

  - And for the girl who let comparison compromise too much, today is the day this story gets a new name (Gen. 35:18).

If you are reading these final words on this last page of our study, I'm so proud of you. You stuck with this thing all the way through. I want you to know that just because our study ends here doesn't mean this is even close to all God wants to teach you about combating comparison in your life. This will be a continual process, one I'm not sure we can ever check off the former struggle list. But if we'll just keep going and becoming all God designed us to be, you'll be you, I'll be me, and she'll be her. Together, we'll all be able to stand before God on that holy day when we meet Him face to face and we can rest. It will be well with our souls.

> When peace, like a river, attendeth my way,
> When sorrows like sea billows roll;
> Whatever my lot, Thou hast taught me to say,
> It is well, it is well with my soul.
> It is well with my soul,
> It is well, it is well with my soul.
>
> Though Satan should buffet, though trials should come,
> Let this blest assurance control,
> That Christ hath regarded my helpless estate,
> And hath shed His own blood for my soul.
>
> My sin—oh, the bliss of this glorious thought!—
> My sin, not in part but the whole,
> Is nailed to the cross, and I bear it no more,
> Praise the Lord, praise the Lord, O my soul!
>
> For me, be it Christ, be it Christ hence to live:
> If Jordan above me shall roll,
> No pang shall be mine, for in death as in life
> Thou wilt whisper Thy peace to my soul.
>
> But, Lord, 'tis for Thee, for Thy coming we wait,
> The sky, not the grave, is our goal;
> Oh, trump of the angel! Oh, voice of the Lord!
> Blessed hope, blessed rest of my soul!
>
> And Lord, haste the day when the faith shall be sight,
> The clouds be rolled back as a scroll;
> The trump shall resound, and the Lord shall descend,
> Even so, it is well with my soul.[1]

Spiritual Gifts Survey

DIRECTIONS

For the last few weeks, you've been discovering who you are as an individual. But now, it's time to discover who God says you are. As someone who follows Jesus, you have a role to play in the building up of His church. This is not a test, so there are no wrong answers.

- *Select the one response you feel best characterizes you, and place that number in the blank provided. Record your answer in the blank beside each item.*

- *Do not spend too much time on any one item. Remember, it is not a test. Usually your immediate response is best.*
- *Please give an answer for each item. Don't skip any items.*
- *Do not ask others how they are answering or how they think you should answer.*
- *Work at your own pace.*

YOUR RESPONSE CHOICES ARE:

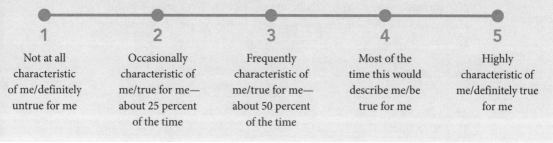

1	2	3	4	5
Not at all characteristic of me/definitely untrue for me	Occasionally characteristic of me/true for me— about 25 percent of the time	Frequently characteristic of me/true for me— about 50 percent of the time	Most of the time this would describe me/be true for me	Highly characteristic of me/definitely true for me

_____ 1. I have the ability to organize ideas, resources, time, and people effectively.

_____ 2. I am willing to study and prepare for the task of teaching or Bible Study.

_____ 3. I am able to relate the truths of God to specific situations.

_____ 4. I often help others grow in their faith.

_____ 5. I find myself able to clearly communicate the truth of salvation.

_____ 6. I have the ability to make difficult decisions when necessary.

_____ 7. I am sensitive to the hurts of other people.

_____ 8. I experience joy in meeting needs through sharing what I have.

_____ 9. I enjoy studying.

_____ 10. I have delivered God's message of warning and judgment.

_____ 11. I am able to sense the true motivation of persons and movements.

_____ 12. I have a special ability to trust God in difficult situations.

_____ 13. I have a strong desire to contribute to the establishment of new churches.

_____ 14. I take action to meet physical and practical needs rather than merely talking about or planning to help.

_____ 15. I enjoy having people over and serving them.

_____ 16. I can adapt my guidance to fit the maturity of those working with me.

_____ 17. I can share and assign meaningful work.

_____ 18. I have an ability and desire to teach.

_____ 19. I am usually able to analyze a situation correctly.

_____ 20. I have a natural tendency to encourage others.

_____ 21. I am willing to take the initiative in helping other Christians grow in their faith.

_____ 22. I have an acute awareness of the emotions of other people, such as loneliness, pain, fear, and anger.

_____ 23. I am a cheerful giver.

_____ 24. I spend time digging into facts.

_____ 25. I feel that I have a message from God to deliver to others.

_____ 26. I can recognize when a person is genuine/honest.

_____ 27. I am a person of vision (a clear mental portrait of a preferable future given by God). I am able to communicate vision in such a way that others commit to making the vision a reality.

_____ 28. I am willing to yield to God's will rather than question and waver.

_____ 29. I would like to be more active in getting the gospel to people in other lands.

_____ 30. It makes me happy to do things for people in need.

_____ 31. I am successful in getting a group to do its work joyfully.

_____ 32. I am able to make strangers feel at ease.

_____ 33. I have the ability to plan learning approaches.

_____ 34. I can identify those who need encouragement.

_____ 35. I have trained Christians to be more obedient disciples of Christ.

_____ 36. I am willing to do whatever it takes to see others come to Christ.

_____ 37. I am attracted to people who are hurting.

_____ 38. I am a generous giver.

_____ 39. I am able to discover new truths.

_____ 40. I have spiritual insights from Scripture concerning issues and people that compel me to speak out.

_____ 41. I can sense when a person is acting in accord with God's will.

_____ 42. I can trust in God even when things look dark.

_____ 43. I can determine where God wants a group to go and help it get there.

_____ 44. I have a strong desire to take the gospel to places where it has never been heard.

_____ 45. I enjoy reaching out to new people in my church and community.

_____ 46. I am sensitive to the needs of people.

_____ 47. I have been able to make effective and efficient plans for accomplishing the goals of a group.

_____ 48. I often am consulted when fellow Christians are struggling to make difficult decisions.

_____ 49. I think about how I can comfort and encourage others in my church.

_____ 50. I am able to give spiritual direction to others.

_____ 51. I am able to present the gospel to lost persons in such a way that they accept the Lord and His salvation.

_____ 52. I possess an unusual capacity to understand the feelings of those in distress.

_____ 53. I have a strong sense of stewardship based on the recognition that God owns all things.

_____ 54. I have delivered to other persons messages that have come directly from God.

_____ 55. I can sense when a person is acting under God's leadership.

_____ 56. I try to be in God's will continually and be available for His use.

_____ 57. I feel that I should take the gospel to people who have different beliefs from me.

_____ 58. I have an awareness of the physical needs of others.

_____ 59. I am skilled in setting forth positive and precise steps of action.

_____ 60. I like to meet visitors at church and make them feel welcome.

_____ 61. I explain Scripture in such a way that others understand it.

_____ 62. I can usually see spiritual solutions to problems.

_____ 63. I welcome opportunities to help people who need comfort, consolation, encouragement, and counseling.

_____ 64. I feel at ease in sharing Christ with nonbelievers.

_____ 65. I can influence others to perform to their highest God-given potential.

_____ 66. I recognize the signs of stress and distress in others.

_____ 67. I desire to give generously and unpretentiously to worthwhile projects and ministries.

_____ 68. I can organize facts into meaningful relationships.

_____ 69. God gives me messages to deliver to His people.

_____ 70. I am able to sense whether people are being honest when they tell of their religious experiences.

_____ 71. I enjoy presenting the gospel to persons of other cultures and backgrounds.

_____ 72. I enjoy doing little things that help people.

_____ 73. I can give a clear, uncomplicated presentation.

_____ 74. I have been able to apply biblical truth to the specific needs of my church.

_____ 75. God has used me to encourage others to live Christlike lives.

_____ 76. I have sensed the need to help other people become more effective in their ministries.

_____ 77. I like to talk about Jesus to those who do not know Him.

_____ 78. I have the ability to make strangers feel comfortable in my home.

_____ 79. I have a wide range of study resources and know how to secure information.

_____ 80. I feel assured that a situation will change for the glory of God even when the situation seem impossible.

SCORING YOUR SURVEY

Follow these directions to figure your score for each spiritual gift.
1. Place in each box your numerical response (1-5) to the item number which is indicated below the box.
2. For each gift, add the numbers in the boxes and put the total in the TOTAL box.

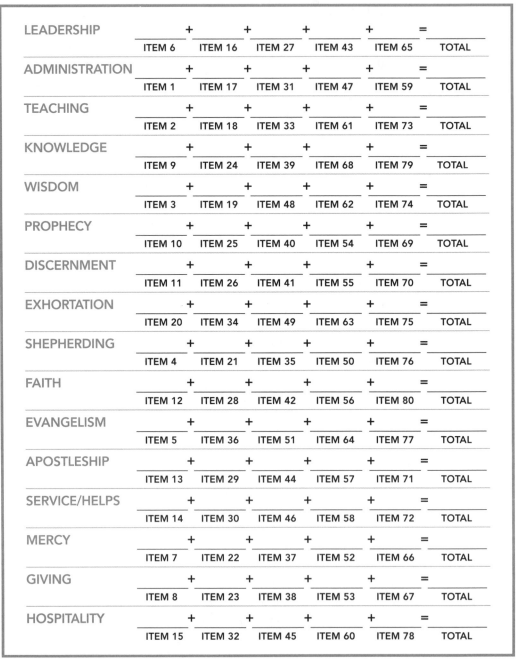

LEADERSHIP ____ + ____ + ____ + ____ = ____
ITEM 6   ITEM 16   ITEM 27   ITEM 43   ITEM 65   TOTAL

ADMINISTRATION ____ + ____ + ____ + ____ = ____
ITEM 1   ITEM 17   ITEM 31   ITEM 47   ITEM 59   TOTAL

TEACHING ____ + ____ + ____ + ____ = ____
ITEM 2   ITEM 18   ITEM 33   ITEM 61   ITEM 73   TOTAL

KNOWLEDGE ____ + ____ + ____ + ____ = ____
ITEM 9   ITEM 24   ITEM 39   ITEM 68   ITEM 79   TOTAL

WISDOM ____ + ____ + ____ + ____ = ____
ITEM 3   ITEM 19   ITEM 48   ITEM 62   ITEM 74   TOTAL

PROPHECY ____ + ____ + ____ + ____ = ____
ITEM 10   ITEM 25   ITEM 40   ITEM 54   ITEM 69   TOTAL

DISCERNMENT ____ + ____ + ____ + ____ = ____
ITEM 11   ITEM 26   ITEM 41   ITEM 55   ITEM 70   TOTAL

EXHORTATION ____ + ____ + ____ + ____ = ____
ITEM 20   ITEM 34   ITEM 49   ITEM 63   ITEM 75   TOTAL

SHEPHERDING ____ + ____ + ____ + ____ = ____
ITEM 4   ITEM 21   ITEM 35   ITEM 50   ITEM 76   TOTAL

FAITH ____ + ____ + ____ + ____ = ____
ITEM 12   ITEM 28   ITEM 42   ITEM 56   ITEM 80   TOTAL

EVANGELISM ____ + ____ + ____ + ____ = ____
ITEM 5   ITEM 36   ITEM 51   ITEM 64   ITEM 77   TOTAL

APOSTLESHIP ____ + ____ + ____ + ____ = ____
ITEM 13   ITEM 29   ITEM 44   ITEM 57   ITEM 71   TOTAL

SERVICE/HELPS ____ + ____ + ____ + ____ = ____
ITEM 14   ITEM 30   ITEM 46   ITEM 58   ITEM 72   TOTAL

MERCY ____ + ____ + ____ + ____ = ____
ITEM 7   ITEM 22   ITEM 37   ITEM 52   ITEM 66   TOTAL

GIVING ____ + ____ + ____ + ____ = ____
ITEM 8   ITEM 23   ITEM 38   ITEM 53   ITEM 67   TOTAL

HOSPITALITY ____ + ____ + ____ + ____ = ____
ITEM 15   ITEM 32   ITEM 45   ITEM 60   ITEM 78   TOTAL

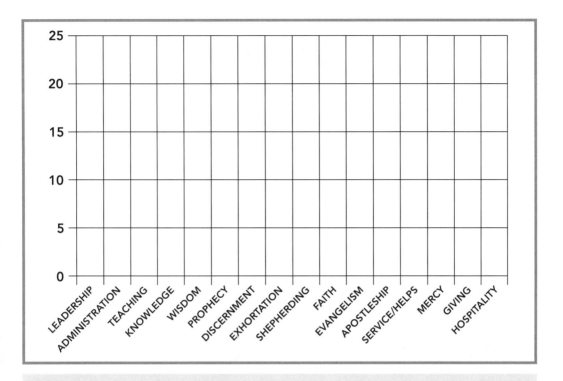

GRAPHING YOUR PROFILE

1. For each gift place a mark across the bar at the point that corresponds to your TOTAL for that gift.

2. For each gift shade the bar below the mark that you have drawn.

3. The resultant graph gives a picture of your gifts. Gifts for which the bars are tall are the ones in which you appear to be strongest. Gifts for which the bars are very short are the ones in which you appear not to be strong.

Now that you have completed the survey, thoughtfully answer the following questions.

The gifts I have begun to discover in my life are:

1. _____

2. _____

3. _____

• After prayer and worship, I am beginning to sense that God wants me to use my spiritual gifts to serve Christ's body by _____.

• I am not sure yet how God wants me to use my gifts to serve others. But I am committed to prayer and worship, seeking wisdom and opportunities to use the gifts I have received from God. Ask God to help you know how He has gifted you for service and how you can begin to use this gift in ministry to others.

ENDNOTES

INTRODUCTION
1. Robert J. Morgan, *Then Sings My Soul* (Nashville: W Publishing, 2011), 184-185.

WEEK ONE
1. Kenneth A. Mathews, *The New American Commentary Genesis: Genesis 11:27-50:26, Volume 1B* (Nashville: Broadman & Holman Publishers, 2005) accessed December 15, 2017 via MyWsb.com.

2. Ibid.

3. James Montgomery Boice, *Genesis: An Expositional Commentary, Volume 2: Genesis 12-36* (Ada, MI: Baker Books, 2006) accessed December 15, 2017 via MyWsb.com.

4. Ibid.

5. *The ESV Study Bible* (Wheaton, IL: Crossway Bibles, 2008), 99.

6. Manfred Mann, "Do Wah Diddy Diddy" in What You Gonna Do? HMV Pop 1320 UK, 1964.

7. Anna Pitts, "You Only Have 7 Seconds To Make a Strong First Impression," *Business Insider,* April 8, 2013, accessed on December 15, 2017. http://www.businessinsider.com/only-7-seconds-tomake-first-impression-2013-4

8. John MacArthur, *The MacArthur Bible Commentary* (Nashville: Thomas Nelson, Inc, 2005), 54.

9. Holman Bible Publishers, *CSB Study Bible* (Nashville: Holman Bible Publishers, 2017), 53, accessed on December 15, 2017 via MyWsb.com.

10. Jeffrey Kranz, "Infographic: Every dream in the Bible (and what they mean)" *Overview Bible,* accessed on December 15, 2017 at https://overviewbible.com/infographic-dreams-bible/

11. Ibid, Mathews.

12. Ibid, Holman Bible Publishers, 53.

13. Ibid, MacArthur, 54.

WEEK TWO
1. Alexis Bennett, "Women Spend on Average, $15,000 on Beauty Products—Here's Proof," *Self,* published March 31, 2017, accessed on December 15, 2017. https://www.self.com/story/amount-of-money-women-spend-onbeauty-products

2. Ezra Sacks, *Wildcats,* directed by Michael Ritchie (1986; Los Angeles, California: Warner Brothers Entertainment).

3. John H. Walton, *The NIV Application Commentary: Genesis* (Grand Rapids, MI: Zondervan, 2001) accessed on December 15, 2017 via MyWsb.com.

4. Timothy Keller, *Counterfeit Gods* (New York: Penguin Books: 2011), 34.

5. Ibid, Mathews.

6. Ibid, Mathews.

7. Ibid, Mathews.

8. Gallagher Flinn, "How Mirrors Work," *How Stuff Works,* accessed on December 15, 2017. https://science.howstuffworks.com/innovation/everyday-innovations/mirror1.htm

9. Ibid, Walton, 569.

10. Emil G. Hirsch, M. Seligsohn, and Executive Committee of the Editorial Board, "Rachel," *Jewish Encyclopedia,* accessed on January 5, 2018. http://www.jewishencyclopedia.com/articles/12521-rachel.

11. Hank Pellissier, "Cousin Marriage – 70% in Pakistan – Should it be Prohibited?" *Institute for Ethics and Emerging Technologies,* May 26, 2012, accessed on January 4, 2018. https://ieet.org/index.php/IEET2/more/pellissier20120526.

12. Ibid

13. Ibid.

14. Ibid.

15. Ibid, Walton, 586.

16. Ibid.

17. Ibid.

18. Ibid, Mathews.

19. Ibid, Walton, 587.

20. Ibid.

21. Chad Brand, Charles Draper, Archie England, Eds. *Holman Illustrated Bible Dictionary* (Nashville: Holman Bible Publishers, 1998).

WEEK THREE

1. "Definition of Affliction," *Dictionary.com*, accessed January 5, 2018 via http://www.dictionary.com/browse/affliction?s=t.

2. "Definition of Reuben," *Blue Letter Bible*, accessed on January 5, 2018 via https://www.blueletterbible.org/lang/lexicon/lexicon.cfm?Strongs=H7205&t=KJV.

3. Definition of Simeon," *Blue Letter Bible*, accessed on January 5, 2018 via https://www.blueletterbible.org/lang/lexicon/lexicon.cfm?Strongs=H8095&t=KJV.

4. "Definition of Simeon," *Blue Letter Bible*, accessed on January 5, 2018 via https://www.blueletterbible.org/lang/lexicon/lexicon.cfm?strongs=H8085&t=KJV.

5. "Definition of Levi," *Blue Letter Bible*, accessed on January 5, 2018 via https://www.blueletterbible.org/lang/lexicon/lexicon.cfm?Strongs=H3878&t=KJV.

6. "Definition of Judah," *Easton's Bible Dictionary via Bible Study Tools*, accessed on January 13, 2018 via https://www.biblestudytools.com/dictionary/judah/.

7. Rochel Chein, "What is the Meaning of the Name 'Jew'?" *Chabad.org*, accessed on January 13, 2018 via http://www.chabad.org/library/article_cdo/aid/640221/jewish/What-is-the-Meaning-of-the-Name-Jew.htm.

8. Franz Delitzsch, *Biblical Commentary on the Prophecies of Isaiah, Volume 1* (Edinburgh: T & T Clark, 1892).

WEEK FOUR

1. "Entry for Mandrake," *New World Encyclopedia*, accessed on January 5, 2018 via http://www.newworldencyclopedia.org/entry/Mandrake_(plant).

2. "Definition for Mandrakes," *Easton's Bible Dictionary via Bible Study Tools,* accessed on January 5, 2018 via https://www.biblestudytools.com/dictionary/mandrakes/.

3. Ibid, *New World Encyclopedia*

4. Ibid.

5. Ibid.

WEEK FIVE

1. Ibid, Mathews.

2. Bruce K. Waltke, *Genesis: A Commentary* (Grand Rapids, MI: Zondervan, 2001).

3. Ibid, Boice.

4. "Definition of Outsiders," *Blue Letter Bible*, accessed on January 5, 2018 via https://www.blueletterbible.org/lang/lexicon/lexicon.cfm?Strongs=H5237&t=KJV.

5. Ibid.

6. Ibid, Mathews.

WEEK SIX

1. Spafford, Horatio G., Lyrics, Bliss, Philip P., Music, "It Is Well With My Soul," *50 Favorites* (Jefferson, OR: Timeless Truths Publications, July 2013), 24.

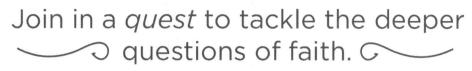

Join in a *quest* to tackle the deeper questions of faith.

6-SESSION STUDY JOURNAL FOR TEEN GIRLS

The Quest

DARING TO KNOW
THE HEART OF GOD

BETH MOORE

LifeWay | Girls

Curiosity is hardwired in humanity. We have this innate need to question and seek after what we don't know or understand. This has been true for all of time: throughout history, we have witnessed the people of God ask questions about who He is, who they are, and how they relate to Him. This is an invitation to embrace the unknown and think through the deeper matters of faith.

In this 6-session Bible study, author and speaker Beth Moore takes girls on a journey through Scripture to explore how God created us to seek after Him. In this lifelong quest of faith, girls will learn to develop intimacy with Him and embrace the adventure that comes with living a life for God.

AVAILABLE PRODUCTS:
- Study Journal | $14.99
- Leader Kit (includes one Study Journal and DVD) | $59.99
- eBook and Digital Leader Kit available at lifeway.com/thequest

Order your copy or view a free sample today! Visit LifeWay.com/TheQuest, stop in to your local LifeWay Store, or call us at 800.458.2772.